Cubby in Wonderland

Cubby in Wonderland

FRANCES JOYCE FARNSWORTH

APPLEWOOD BOOKS
Publishers of America's Living Past
CARLISLE, MASSACHUSETTS

ISBN: 978-1-4290-9318-7

Thank you for purchasing an Applewood book.
Applewood reprints America's lively classics—
books from the past that are still of
interest to modern readers.
Our mission is to build a picture of America
through its primary sources.

To inquire about this edition
or to request a free copy
of our current catalog
featuring our best-selling books, write to:
Applewood Books
P.O. Box 27
Carlisle, MA 01741
For more complete listings,
visit us on the web at:
www.awb.com

Manufactured in the United States of America

Publisher's Note

Applewood Books is pleased to present reprints of the charming Cubby books, written by Riverton, Wyoming author Frances Joyce Farnsworth (1881-1962). These classic books, set in Yellowstone and Grand Teton, were written in the 1930s. People have learned a lot since then on safe ways to enjoy the National Parks and coexist with wildlife. These cozy stories of a baby bear and his loving parents are a window on the past—a time, even, when people fed bears from their cars. These practices are no longer allowed, because we know more about appropriate bear safety, especially when it comes to keeping a proper distance from wildlife and making sure food and garbage are stored in a bear-proof manner.

Enjoy this book about Cubby for its warmth and kindness and remember to follow these basic rules:

- Do not approach wildlife.
- Stay at least 100 yards (91M) away from bears and wolves.
- When viewing bears along roads, use pullouts and stay in your car.
- Keep all food and garbage stored in a bear-proof manner.

For more information on Bear Safety, please visit:
www.nps.gov/yell/planyourvisit/bearsafety.htm
or
www.nps.gov/grte/planyourvisit/bearsafety.htm

CUBBY IN WONDERLAND

TO

KATE BARCLAY FARNSWORTH

IN MEMORY

OF HAPPY DAYS TOGETHER

IN

YELLOWSTONE WONDERLAND

CONTENTS

ILLUSTRATIONS

CHAPTER I

THE DENS OF THE TWO-LEGGED TRIBE

"I'M thinking of taking you on a trip this summer," said Mommie Bear, as she peered out of her cave in Grand Teton Mountain.

"Oh, goody," said Cubby, happily, "I'd love to travel. Where are we going?"

"I think we'll go over toward the Yellowstone Park, Cubby." Mommie Bear wisely rubbed her nose with a great paw. "Last summer I met a bear who said there was nice fishing to be had and that the two-legged tribe was kind to all of our family."

"But, Mother," said Cubby, "we'll miss our mountains, and our pretty looking-glass lakes."

"Maybe we will find some just as good," smiled his mother, "and anyway, we'll see what we shall see. How about it, Cubby? Don't you want to go? You know we can turn around and come back whenever we want to."

Cubby chuckled a funny little bear chuckle. "Do I *want* to go? *Do* I want to? Don't tease me, Mommie Bear. I want to go so much that I can hardly keep from dancing. When do we start?"

"We'll start right away. We want to be in time for the tourist season."

"What's that?" asked Cubby.

11

"It's something about the two-legged tribe," said Mommie Bear. "Every summer when the snow is gone and the paths are cleared, the two-legged tribe comes in great crowds to look at the Park. They have a nice time, I'm told. And they like everything—even bears!"

"It sounds jolly," said Cubby. "When do we go?"

"I think we should start right away," said Mommie Bear. "It will take us longer to get there than it does the two-legged tribe. You see, they have automobiles."

"What's an—?" Cubby couldn't say the word.

"It's a sort of an animal, I guess," said Mommie Bear. "They ride on its back. It goes rushing along their trails making the funniest whistles and toots as it rounds the curves. That friendly bear told me about them."

"It sounds jolly," said Cubby again. "When *do* we start?"

"I think we should start right away," said Mommie Bear.

And so they started. Mommie Bear led the way. "I think, Cubby," she said, "that you may learn a great deal. I want you to look around as we move along and ask me about anything you do not understand. We are starting early so we will have time to make the most of our trip."

Mommie Bear and Cubby went on together. Sometimes they sat down and slid over snowy banks. It was fun. As much fun as the little two-legged cubs have with their sleds. There were such splendid long slides! Mommie Bear knew just how to pick the way that was the safest and the best. Cubby in his fine fur coat was as snug as he could be.

It took several days to come down from their home high up on the great mountain, but at last they reached the bottom and looked up.

"Whew!" cried Cubby. "Did we live up there, Mommie Bear? Away up there? It's so high! it—takes my breath away! Will it be as much fun going up as it was coming down?"

Mommie Bear laughed. "I think we will not try it for some time," she said. "I've heard of steam-heated dens over in the Yellowstone, and that's where I mean to spend my next winter."

"Steam-heated?" cried Cubby. "What is steam and what is heated?"

"I don't exactly know myself, sonny. But it's all warm and snug and cozy. We'll find out more about it when we get there."

"It does sound jolly," said Cubby. "Let's keep going."

Mommie Bear broke a hole in the ice and fished out a few nice fish for their supper.

As they were jogging along next morning, all of a sudden Cubby cried: "Do look, Mommie Bear! What are those things? Are they little mountains?"

Mommie Bear looked, and then she laughed and she laughed and she laughed. "Oh, Cubby," she cried when she could speak out loud, "those are not mountains.

They're dens—the two-legged tribe's dens. But come along, sonny, maybe we can see what they are like inside."

So Cubby and Mommie Bear went to peep into the windows of the lodges and the cabins that were cuddled down together at the foot of the lake with the great old Tetons standing guard overhead.

Cubby had to stand on his hind legs, but he was used to that. "Well, well," said he, "who ever saw such queer looking things?"

"Those long things are tables," said Mommie wisely, "and those other things are called chairs. The two-leggers like to sit in them."

Cubby and Mommie Bear went to peep into the windows

"How funny!" said Cubby.

"They do have queer ways," Mommie replied. "Why, they even build fires right in their dens!"

"Fires!" exclaimed Cubby, horrified.

"Yes, fires. But they build them in the fireplace.

You see that one over there? Once when I was a little bear and quite curious, I peeped into one of these dens while on a trip with my mother—no, not here, Cubby— and I saw a father and mother two-legger with their little ones sitting around the fireplace watching the red flames as they danced up the chimney. You wouldn't believe how nice and cozy it looked."

"Maybe that's what they call a steam-heated den," said Cubby.

"I don't know about that," replied Mommie Bear. "We'll find out later."

"I'd like to see the little two-leggers," said Cubby a bit wistfully. "Do you suppose they will like me, Mommie Bear?"

"Listen," said Mommie Bear, seriously. "Don't worry about their liking you. If you like others and are kind and good, they'll like you too."

"Then I'm going to like 'em," said Cubby, happily.

"We will be moving on," said Mommie Bear. "I think we'll take the two-legged folks' trail now. It's quite nice and smooth."

CHAPTER II

MEETING MR. MOOSE

"WHIST," said Cubby. "What's that? Something is coming. Look, Mommie Bear; it's a tree and it's walking around!"

Mommie Bear looked. And then Mommie Bear laughed. She sat down in a great heap of soft snow and laughed until two great bear tears trickled down her cheeks. "Cubby," she said, "there is so much for you to do and see, so much for you to learn. And it's going to be the most fun to show you all about the world. That does look like a tree moving around. But it isn't. That's Mr. Moose!"

And then Cubby looked again and he saw it wasn't a tree at all. It was an animal with great branches on its head.

"Oh," said Cubby, in surprise. "It must be very hard to have to carry all that around. Can't he ever take them off, Mommie Bear, and rest himself?"

"Oh, yes, he takes them off," said Mommie Bear. "Every year he takes them off and throws them away and a new one grows in their place. I suppose he rests his head then—but he isn't really happy, for he hides himself away while they grow again."

"Well," sighed Cubby, "I'm glad I don't have to carry trees around with me."

"They're horns, or antlers," said Mommie Bear. "They are hard like teeth. Let's go and talk with him, Cubby."

Mr. Moose was quite surprised to see Mrs. Bear and Cubby. "Why, good morning, Mrs. Bear," he said, "I didn't know that you had awakened from your long winter's nap. Aren't you early this spring?"

"Perhaps I am," said Mommie Bear; "it does seem as if the days were a mite shorter than they were last year when I wakened. I had a good nap and I woke up feeling fine. How's everything with you, Mr. Moose? Was it a hard winter?"

Mr. Moose

"Well, no," said Mr. Moose, "not very good nor very bad. We always found plenty of food and shelter. Everyone in our family is feeling pretty comfortable this spring."

"That's great," said Mommie Bear. "Cubby and I have made up our minds to see Yellowstone Park this summer. Thought we would start early."

"That's a fine idea," said Mr. Moose. "I think I shall spend some time in the Park myself. There are so many deep thickets and other places where one is never bothered."

"Perhaps I'll be seeing you then," said Mommie Bear. "Next time Cubby will know you. Just now he thought you were a tree! Where is Mrs. Moose? I wish Cubby could meet her too."

"Oh, she is back with the herd. I came on ahead to look about and see if there were any better feeding grounds to be had."

"And have you a little Cub?" asked Cubby, a bit shyly.

Mr. Moose looked very puzzled for a moment and then he smiled. "Oh, I see," he said. "We call our little ones calves instead of cubs. The calves stay with their mothers, just as you do. So you didn't know me, little fellow? Would you like me to tell you something about myself?"

"Oh, I'd love it," said Cubby.

"I am the largest of a family known as the deer family. Some of my relations are very small. One of them is the kind of a deer that Santa Claus drives. Do you know about Santa, Cubby?"

"Oh, yes," said Cubby; "who doesn't? And he drives —he drives the reindeer!"

"Yes, sir," said Mr. Moose, "that is exactly what he drives, and they are my cousins. I had a race once with a bear. He was like you, Cubby, and thought I could never run with all these branches on my head. We had a jolly time. It does look as if they would catch in the branches of the trees. But see, I can lay them flat against my back—like this—and then I can run very

fast. I showed him then how useful the great shovels
on my horns could be."

"Useful?" said Cubby, in surprise. "Whatever can
you do with them?"

"Look," said Mr. Moose, and he bent his head and
scooped up a great shovelful of snow with his horns!

"They make a regular snowplow," he chuckled. "And
when the plants are covered with snow I can easily dig it
away to find my food. I remember"—and he laughed—
"I scooped up the snow—like this—and threw it all over
Mr. Bear." And with that he scooped up a shovelful
and tossed it on Cubby.

It came tumbling down on Cubby's furry little brown
head. It got into his eyes and his ears, but he was such
a good-natured little bear that he just laughed until he
could laugh no longer. As he scrambled out of the
snow he looked up at big Mr. Moose. "Do it again,"
he cried.

"Not to-day," said Mr. Moose. "I think that is
enough for this time. I just wanted to show you how
my antlers work. Trees can't do that, can they?"

"What did Mr. Bear say?" asked Cubby.

"Why he just laughed, as you did, and thought it a
great joke. He thought I could not swim. Some day
I'll show you, Cubby."

"Do you really swim?"

"Indeed I do," said Mr. Moose. "Some warm days
I lie for hours in the water with only my nose sticking
out."

"And your horns," said Cubby, "whatever do you do with them?"

"I take them right with me," said Mr. Moose.

"And didn't Mr. Bear find anything that he could do that you could not?"

"Yes, he did," said Mr. Moose, honestly. "There are several things he could do that I cannot. Now I never live in a den. I wouldn't be comfortable to crawl into a hole. And I never, never could sleep all winter. He didn't think of those two things but he thought of something else. Mr. Bear can stand up and even walk around on his hind legs, and I am not made so that I can do that. He showed me how he could hug a tree!"

"I wish you would tell me whether I am out earlier this spring or you are keeping your antlers later than usual," asked Mommie Bear. "It seems to me that there is something strange about it."

"There is," said Mr. Moose. "There is something very strange about it. It may be that you are out earlier than usual, but I am certainly keeping my antlers later than usual too. In fact, mine are the last pair of antlers in the herd. The others lost theirs weeks ago. I have worried about it. But I really would like to keep them. It's a nuisance to have to grow a new pair every year."

"I suppose it is," agreed Mommie Bear. "But I am glad Cubby could see them. It will be fine if you can keep them."

Mr. Moose nodded his head. And then a strange thing happened. One of his great antlers fell from his head! In silence Cubby and Mommie Bear with big Mr. Moose stood looking at the monstrous horn as it lay upon the snow. It was almost a yard in length and a foot in width. Mr. Moose was the first to speak.

"It's happened!" he sighed. "Now I must be moving on." He seemed to have forgotten Mommie Bear and Cubby. It was as if he were talking to himself. "I'll not go back to the herd. They'd laugh at me. I'll hide away for awhile. I do feel so light headed." He moved away into the forest.

"I'm sorry," said Cubby. "It was such a wonderful antler."

"No need to be sorry," said his Mommie. "He'll lose the other in a day or two. After all, Mother Nature knows what is best for her children."

CHAPTER III

MRS. OTTER'S GAME

MOMMIE BEAR showed Cubby how to find just the right kind of food to make him grow big and strong. When night came, they always found a snug place in which to sleep, under a great rock or deep in the bushes that were still covered with snow. And there, snuggly cuddled in the long thick fur close to Mommie's warm body, Cubby would beg for a bedtime story. Mommie Bear knew the most wonderful stories for Mommie Bear had seen much of the world. Cubby could hardly wait to see it all for himself.

In the morning when they crept out of their warm little house they would find the world all white and glittering. The sun made the snowy mountaintops turn to pink with its first bright rays of light. Cubby would blink his little eyes, it was so dazzling.

"It will not always be so," Mommie Bear told him. "Soon the snow will melt and the grass will be green. Then the flowers will bloom, wonderful flowers, lilies of red, and larkspur deep purple, and pink wild roses."

"Oh, then it will be beautiful just the same," said Cubby, eagerly. "I was afraid when the snow was gone there would be nothing pretty left."

"Just you wait," said Mommie Bear. "We'll find

some of the prettiest flowers in the world. And the flowers are sweet, and the bees know how to make something good from them."

"What, Mommie?" asked Cubby.

"Wait and see," said Mommie Bear. "We'll keep that for a little surprise. Let's enjoy the snow while it lasts. Come here, sonny, look back toward our Teton Mountains."

"How high they hold their heads!" said Cubby.

"Always they hold the snow in their high canyons," Mommie Bear said, softly. "And they wear their snow coats far into the summer. Wild animals love them. It is as if they held out their arms to us and said: 'Come, all you wild things, come and live with me. I will take care of you. I have homes for you on my steep, rocky walls. Come, wild things, live with me.'"

"It does seem as if I can just feel them saying that," said Cubby, happily.

"We will go back to them some day," Mommie Bear said, as if to herself. "They seem to call me. And I'm glad to know they are there. After all, Cubby, the mountains, our mountains, are wild things like ourselves. Nothing can tame the grand old Tetons! They stand there so rugged and strong, just as the Great Father made them."

"It's nice to know they will be there when we come back to them," said Cubby. "It's nice to know that they keep us safe. But, Mommie Bear, will we be safe in the Park?"

"Just as safe as we can be, Cubby. Uncle Sam keeps us safe in the Park."

"And what is Uncle Sam?" asked Cubby. "Is that a mountain too?"

"No, Cubby. I don't know what it is. Uncle Sam belongs to the two-legged tribe. Uncle Sam says the bears and all the animals are safe in the Park. All we have to do is to behave ourselves and everything will be all right. Now we are coming to Lewis Lake. Look, Cubby, the trees are gone. Once there was a fire here. You know I've always told you, Cubby, that fire is a dangerous thing. Forest fires are very bad. Whenever you smell smoke you must run from it."

"What does it smell like?"

"You will know it. It burns your nose and makes your eyes smart so that the tears come. It always means trouble in a forest. I'm glad bears don't carry matches so no one can ever blame us for starting a fire. The two-leggers use matches, but they know they have to be careful. When they build a fire to cook their food, they always put out every little spark before they go away. It's the only safe thing to do."

"If I ever see a spark, I'll put it out too," said Cubby.

"Be careful," said Mommie Bear; "sparks burn and a burn hurts. But do look who is here. Why, how do you do, Mrs. Otter? I declare I haven't seen you in a long, long time. This is my little Cubby, Mrs. Otter. We are going to stay in the Park this summer."

"Well, well," said Mrs. Otter, "isn't that fine! Cubby

will have a great time. Spring is on the way and all this snow and ice will soon be gone. It's getting pretty soft now."

"That's right," said Mommie Bear. "I've been telling Cubby about the flowers that would be coming soon."

Mrs. Otter held up a foot and looked at her webbed toes with

Mrs. Otter

their curved, blunt claws. That's so," she said. "And I'll have to bring my babies down and teach them to swim. It's funny, Mrs. Bear, but I always have to teach them how. I love to swim. I'm just made for swimming. You see this close, thick fur of mine turns the water and my long, slim body glides through it. But—would you believe it?—those babies almost cry when I try to take them into the water."

"They'll like it once they learn," said Mommie Bear, wisely. "I suppose it does frighten them a little at first. I'll have to teach Cubby, here, about swimming and climbing."

"I have five to teach," said Mrs. Otter. A happy otter smile came on her face. "Five of the sweetest little baby otters anyone ever saw. I left them a few minutes ago to come out for a little food and exercise. I've a nice home in a cavern right by the water's edge. I found it last fall already made for me."

"Is the fishing good?" asked Mommie Bear.

"Quite good for this season," said Mrs. Otter.

"I guess we will stay here awhile then," said Mommie Bear, "and wait until the snow is gone and the tourist season starts. Cubby and I have our hearts set on seeing a lot this summer."

"Well, I have never been farther than over to the Thumb," said Mrs. Otter, "but it is as good as a circus to see so many of those funny creatures called people."

"Is that what they call them?" Mommie Bear's voice was filled with surprise. "Listen, Cubby, they call the two-legged tribe, people. People—its a funny name, isn't it!"

"People," said Cubby, "people!"

"Yes," said Mrs. Otter, "that's what I thought. There are big people and little people and fat people and slim people and white people and red people and brown people—and I saw one yellow people!"

"Good," nodded Mommie Bear. "After all, they are much like bears. There are white bears, black bears, brown bears, and even yellowish bears. I really feel as if I begin to understand people."

"They are very interesting," went on Mrs. Otter.

"It is such fun watching them, it is really. They run around and look at things and have such queer voices. Some of their voices are very deep and some are very high and some are just middle-sized. They laugh a great deal and have a wonderful time."

"I'm so glad we have come," said Mommie Bear. "We'll just wait here until fine weather comes and then we will go along with the people and have a nice time with them."

"Then make yourself at home, Mrs. Bear," said Mrs. Otter. "There's plenty of fish for all. Can Cubby go with me? I'm going to play awhile on that nice hillside yonder. I've a very special game that I can only play while the snow lasts."

"Thanks, Mrs. Otter," said Mommie Bear. "I know Cubby will love to learn a new game, and I'll catch some fish while you two are gone. Have a good time, Cubby, and remember your manners."

"I will, Mommie," said Cubby.

"I was so afraid I'd not have another chance to play my game this year," said Mrs. Otter, happily, as she trotted up the hillside. "Of course I could leave the babies and go high up on the mountainside and find snow later, but I don't think I really should. Cubby, do you like to slide?"

"Yes," said Cubby, "Mommie and I tried it coming down the mountain."

"Well, I do too, I just love to slide," said Mrs. Otter. "It's almost more fun than swimming. Do you want to

know what my game is? I play I'm a bird. Don't tell
your mother; she might think I'm silly. But I find a
steep slope like this and then I slide down it. If I do it
over and over, it gets quite slick. Ooooooh—when I go
so fast, it's just like flying! Sometimes I think the gulls
that fly over the lake would like to do it if they could.
The cold snow feels so fresh and good. Here's my slide.
Now watch me!"

Mrs. Otter dropped down on the smooth little path
and went flashing down, head first!

Cubby just dropped over backward with laughter,
and then a funny thing happened! He had sat down in
Mrs. Otter's slide—and down, down, down he went like
a flash! He found himself, in no time, at the foot of the
slope with Mrs. Otter!

"Isn't it grand!" cried Mrs. Otter, her eyes glittering.

"Come on," said Cubby, "let's do it again!"

CHAPTER IV

A FRIEND — THE RANGER

ONE day as Mommie Bear and Cubby were sitting together by the lake Mommie Bear suddenly raised her head. She sat very still. She seemed to be listening. Cubby watched her. He knew that she was puzzled. He wondered if she were pleased. He knew that he should wait quietly until she spoke to him. So he waited.

And then Mommie Bear turned to Cubby. "Cubby," she whispered, "there is something in the air. Do you smell it?"

Cubby began to sniff. He drew in long, deep breaths. Yes, there was something. It was different, and yet it was not unpleasant. It did not frighten him. "What is it, mother?" he asked.

"It is the wind's message," said Mommie Bear. "The wind is blowing toward us from something coming nearer. It is one of the two-legged tribe, one of the creatures that Mrs. Otter calls people."

"Maybe it's a tourist," said Cubby.

But Mommie Bear shook her head. "Not yet, Cubby, it's someone else. I wish Mrs. Otter would come along and tell us. Let's move along through these bushes and see if we can find her." So Mommie Bear with Cubby at

29

her heels moved along quietly through the bushes. At last they found Mrs. Otter. She had just come up out of the water, where she had been swimming. Mommie Bear told her of the wind's message.

"Oh," said Mrs. Otter, "that's just our friend. I've known him for years. He's one of the people who live in the Park and look after us. Every once in awhile he comes along to see that everything is all right. I tell you he wouldn't let anyone set any traps or do anything to hurt any wild animal in the Park. That is one of the nicest things about living here. We're so safe and well-cared for. Sometimes he throws out a bit of food for us when the winter is very cold."

"Isn't that nice?" said Mommie Bear. "The more I hear about Yellowstone Park the better I like it. I hope we get acquainted with your friend this summer. But just now Cubby and I will stay behind these bushes and watch him pass."

"They call him the Ranger," said Mrs. Otter. "There are several of them who stay in the Park all winter. I visited a cousin of mine one springtime and there was a different one over where she lives, but he was just as nice as this one."

"Oh, look," said Cubby, "there he goes. Why, he walks standing up just like bears do sometimes! Only he doesn't stoop. My, doesn't he carry himself beautifully! What are those things on his feet?"

"They are snowshoes," said Mrs. Otter. "Sometimes he wears them and sometimes he doesn't. I guess he can put them on and off. It must be handy. He can walk right over great drifts of snow and not slip down. Sometimes he wears a long, thin strip of something on his feet. They call them skis. Then he seems to almost fly over the ice and snow."

"I think he is splendid," said Cubby. "If I were a little people instead of a little bear, I'd want to be a Ranger when I grew up. I wonder if he knows how much all the little bears and otter babies and everything else, out here, like him?"

"He has lots of friends," said Mrs. Otter, "and he gets well acquainted with all the wild things in the Park. I suppose a Ranger sees things that we do, and knows more about our ways than any other people in the world. He's kind to us."

"He's my friend too," said Cubby.

"Yes," said Mommie Bear, slowly. "It's real comfortable to come to a place like this where one has friends. I know I'm going to like it."

CHAPTER V

MEETING THE TOURISTS

THE days grew longer. The sun shone brighter. Bit by bit the snow melted and disappeared. At last the ice in the lake was gone. The water lay smooth under the blue sky with the sun making sparkles in the ripples.

Everyone felt it. The time had come. The flowers blossomed on the mountainsides and the little streams sang as they hurried on their way.

"We'll be getting on," said Mommie Bear. "Come, sonny." But he was almost afraid. There was so much to see and know.

"Come, sonny," said his mother again, gently. "We'll just go along quietly until we learn the way of it all."

And so they set out. But they kept back from the great roadway. It was all so new and strange—just yet. A long climb lay ahead, but they trudged on together.

"Listen," said Cubby one day, and his eyes grew big and bright. "It's the tourists! I hear them coming riding in their cars." Mrs. Otter had explained about the automobiles. "Let's wait here awhile and peep through the branches."

So they waited and they saw the people riding along. It was fun to hear the honking on the curves. "They go so fast," said Cubby. "But I don't suppose they have all summer as we do, have they, Mommie Bear?"

"Maybe not," she answered. "We can take all the time we need to see it all. But, of course, we have to find our food, and that takes time too."

Day by day they moved on a bit farther, and day by day they grew a bit braver until, at last, they were very near the roadside when the cars passed by.

And one day they met one of their relations. He was a big black bear, sitting by the roadside like a nice big black dog. He wasn't surprised to see Mommie Bear and Cubby although they were surprised to see him.

"No," he told them, with a yawn, "I'm not surprised to see you. I'm not surprised to see anything or anyone. One sees so much, sitting here by the road. I've been here since daylight, and now I am so full and so sleepy I guess I'll have to take a nap."

"When do you eat?" said Mommie Bear. "Cubby and I watch a good bit and listen, but it takes a lot of time to find our food."

The big black bear shook his big black head. "Where," he asked, "are you from? Oh," he went on when they had told him, "I knew you were from the back country. You've a lot to learn. The people who go by in the cars love us. Yes, they love us. If you'll just sit here and look pleasant, you will be fed all day long. And with that cute little cub, well, I guess they will give you anything you want. They'll be wild about him. But go on a little farther, for if you stop here they'll give it all to you and I'll not have anything."

"It's very strange," said Mommie Bear. "I never have heard anything like it. We'll go on. And—well—Cubby and I will think it over."

So they hurried on and talked it over together. "I don't know what to do," Mommie Bear told Cubby. "It sounds so nice and friendly, but I'm not used to it. Shall we try it now or shall we wait?"

"Let's try," said Cubby. So they found a nice, shady place and sat down beside the road to wait.

Cubby sniffed. "They're coming," he whispered. Mommie Bear nodded. Cubby edged closer to Mommie Bear. And then around the corner came the car! Cubby's feet would not stand still! They simply ran away with him. Then he heard voices.

"Oh, mother, look, a darling little cub bear! Oh, daddy, stop, please do!"

Cubby heard the grinding of the brakes. He wondered if they had something for him. But he kept on running. When at last his feet stopped and he turned around, there was Mommie Bear right behind him! He looked up into her eyes and then they both began to laugh.

"Oh," cried Cubby, "why did I have to run away? But I couldn't help it. Something made me do it."

"I know all about it," said Mommie Bear, "something made me run too. I don't know what it was. I just had to. I didn't dream you could run so fast, Cubby, darling."

"We'll try it again," said Cubby. "If we keep trying, we can do it." But whenever they thought of how they had run away they laughed and laughed and laughed.

"Now we'll have to hunt our supper," said Mommie Bear, "but it serves us right. Those people did want to see you so much and we were really quite rude. We won't run next time, I feel sure."

They slept hidden away in a nice hollow under a tree that night and found their breakfast the next morning before going to the highway. Soon they found a nice place and again sat down to wait for the tourists.

It was not long until the wind brought a message to them, and the sound of motors drifted through the air. Then they saw something very strange—great, low, yellow things, moving on wheels. There were one, two, three, four of them. Mommie Bear stood up and Cubby with wide eyes watched them coming.

"This is no place for us," said Mommie Bear, softly. "Let's go, Cubby, dear," and they shuffled off into the forest.

"Look out," said a voice. "Why don't you look where you are going?"

"Oh, I beg your pardon," said Mommie Bear. "I was —well, I was rather startled." She looked down at a little furry creature at her feet, a woodchuck.

"Startled at what?"

"Why, at all those monstrous yellow things on the road. Cubby and I have almost grown used to the cars but these great things—they are alarming!"

"And you are a bear!" said the woodchuck. "I do declare. I didn't suppose bears were afraid of anything. Most of the bears in the park are not afraid of anything. They go around as if they owned it. I don't see why the people let them, but they seem to like it. Where are you from?"

"We came from over the mountains," said Mommie Bear, "and we are not yet used to the ways of the Park. Are you quite sure that we would be safe out by the road when those great yellow things go by?"

"Safe? Let me tell you. Those are the Yellow Park buses. People who do not have cars of their own go in the buses. They're very kind people too. They just love to see a little cub bear. They'd make a real fuss over you. Next time wait. Lots of nice things happen here."

"Thanks a lot," said Mommie Bear. "It's good of you to tell us all about these things. We feel so new and strange. And we do so want to get acquainted. We'll be going on now. Come, Cubby."

The next time that Cubby and his mother waited for the cars by the roadside they did not run away. It was quite breath-taking to see the two-legged tribe so very, very near. But they waited, although they trembled. And Cubby did not jump to grab the cooky that was thrown to him. He just stood waiting and looking. The people in the car laughed and talked, but his head was in such a whirl that he hardly heard a word.

But when the car drove on there were many nice bits of food to be picked up. Some of the things were dif-

ferent from anything Cubby had ever tasted before—
but he liked them!

"It's sweet," said Mommie Bear, "and that reminds
me, Cubby, that before very long we'll find what the
bees make from the flowers."

Cubby just stood waiting and looking

"I can hardly wait," said Cubby, but just then
another car drove up and stopped to see the "dear little
cub" and its mother. And when they went on there was
more to be eaten.

And so it went on through the day. Cubby forgot to
feel frightened when a car stopped. He looked into
the faces of the people and found them friendly faces.
And so he went nearer and nearer the cars, but his
mother stayed far away at the edge of the road. She did
not find it as easy to make friends as did Cubby.

"Watch out," said a man who sat at the wheel. "That mother bear seems timid. She isn't an old hand at the Park. Don't take any chances of going between her and her cub. All this is new to her and she doesn't take to it like the little fellow."

"I like her," said the lady. "I like to see the big bears stay back rather than come too near. And, see—the little fellow is taking some of the food to his mother. That's thoughtful of him."

Mommie Bear smiled to herself. "After all, the people understood her pretty well. It was rather wonderful! It was just like having a party, and the company kept coming. But she didn't like it when they took out a black box that opened up and stuck out its head. It had one bright eye. When they pointed it at Cubby, Mommie Bear made a low growl in her throat. And the box was put away quickly. The people said they guessed "Mother Bear didn't want them to take the cub's picture," whatever that meant.

At night when they found their bed, Mommie Bear said: "It's all very well, Cubby; but if we sit here and eat all summer, we will never get through the Park and see all the things that we set out to see. Shall we wait and just get big and fat and lazy like that big black bear we passed or shall we go on?"

They decided to go on and were surprised the next morning to find how near they were to the first place of interest.

CHAPTER VI

THE PAINT POTS

WHEN Mommie Bear and Cubby reached West Thumb — a funny name, Cubby thought—they found a lot of people there. A strange odor was in the air. Here and there rose little puffs of something white.

Mommie Bear was puzzled. "Now, follow me, Cubby," she warned, "and don't you turn to the right or the left. There's something strange here, I can tell you." Mommie Bear stepped carefully, for the ground was slippery and warm.

Just beyond a fence lay something that looked as if it were alive, for it moved. It seemed to rise and fall, but it wasn't water, it was mud, bright-colored mud, boiling just like thick mush in a pot over a fire. "Do you suppose it's good to eat?" whispered Cubby. "Don't you think we might taste it?"

"You'd burn your tongue," said Mommie Bear. "It's hot—awfully hot. Look how it bubbles and spatters. But it's pretty. There must be something hot under the ground to make it boil so."

"It's a pretty pink," said Cubby, "and over yonder are lovely shades of green."

"I thought I'd seen a great deal," said Mommie Bear,

"but I have never seen anything like this before. I—I didn't know there was anything like this. Perhaps, if we listen, we'll hear the people tell something about it." So they listened.

"There are larger Paint Pots in the Park than these," a man said to a lady near by, "but none more beautifully colored. I'd like to have a specimen of that mud, but you are not allowed to carry things from the Park."

"It's a good thing," said the lady; "there wouldn't be any mud left if they permitted it; and then people would be burned trying to get it. It's wonderful as it is right there. My, but there are a lot of strange things here! Do look at that steaming thing yonder."

"Paint Pots! That's a good name," said Mommie Bear as she and Cubby stood and looked and looked and looked. People came and people went, but they were more interested in the strange things of nature than they were in the bears. Cubby was glad. He did not want to be bothered just then. He wanted to look and look and look.

Sometimes he put out a furry little paw. But he drew it back. Of course it wasn't alive even if it did move, but it certainly was hot, and how it did bubble! Here and there were little baby bubblers having a jolly time by themselves.

"Look at this tiny one," said Cubby; "it puffs up its cheeks very high and then says 'Woof.' It must be a little cub bubbler. I love the pretty colors. They look as if they had been taken from the sunset."

"Listen to the funny noises they make as they bubble, Cubby," said Mommie Bear.

"It sounds as if someone were chuckling down under the ground. Perhaps it's a fairy who lives in a great den deep under the earth, and maybe the steam, like smoke, comes from his fire that keeps him snug and warm away down there where the sun can never shine. But it is a fine den and he likes it."

"What a nice little story you are making, Cubby!" said his mother.

"And one day," Cubby went on, happily, "he thought that it would be nice to make something interesting for the people and the bears to see. So he took the colors from the sunset and mixed up a lot of mud pies and put them on his roof. The heat from his house made them run together and turn into magic mud that bubbled and danced. Every once in a while they would make a big, big bubble, and then one could hear the fairy laughing and chuckling down in his snug, warm den deep, deep in the ground."

"He had such a nice time," went on Mommie Bear, taking up the story, "that all his relations came to live with him, and they made themselves nice little homes too, with pretty roofs that let the heat and steam pass through. Even the little cub fairies made their little wee cub roofs. It was so pretty and so odd that everyone loved to come and see. Even little Cubby and his Mommie from over the mountains liked to come and watch the bubbly roofs of the fairy houses."

"I wonder if we shall find anything else as beautiful?" asked Cubby, as at last they started on.

"I wouldn't be surprised at anything," said Mommie Bear. "I have heard the Yellowstone Park called a wonderland, and I think it is. One wonders what lovely thing will come next."

CHAPTER VII

MRS. PELICAN'S FISH BASKET

"WHAT a lovely lake!" exclaimed Cubby. "That is Yellowstone Lake," said Mommie Bear. "It is a very large lake to be so high in the mountains. I will have to see if there are any fish to be had from it. But, see—there is a man fishing now! He has a nice string of trout. We must be very quiet."

"Oh, Mommie, look out on the water!" cried Cubby.

"Hush," said Mommie Bear. "But I do declare! Why—why those boats are alive! Look at that one running along out there by itself. It says put-put-put-put!"

"Alive!" screamed a big gray bird. "Ha, ha!" Cubby and his Mommie were quite startled. "Those are motor boats. They have something on them that makes them run that way."

"Well, it is all very strange," said Mommie Bear. "Dear me, we thought you were a stone, you were so quiet."

"I'm a gull," said the bird, "and sometimes I'm quite noisy. I like to come to the Yellowstone. It's so cool and pleasant and there is plenty to eat. Even the people are interesting. A lot of my relations come here for the summer. Your baby there must get a peep at Mrs. Pelican. He will be interested. She is an odd bird!"

"So that is what you call me," called a voice from the sky.

Cubby and Mommie Bear looked up. And dropping down over their heads was the most enormous bird! Cubby ducked for shelter.

There was a swishing of wings and then before them stood Mrs. Pelican. She was so big and so awkward. One could hardly believe that she could fly so high and so gracefully. She grinned a pelican grin. "I know," she chuckled, "that I'm not very handsome on land. My legs are too short. But up in the air it's different."

Mrs. Pelican

"Where," asked Cubby, stepping forward bravely, "did you ever find that funny thing you are carrying in your mouth?"

Mrs. Pelican laughed and then she said: "That's my bill, young man. It grows right on me just as your fur grows on you. And am I proud of it? Indeed I am. I don't believe any bird in all the world has a finer one. It's more than a bill—it's my fish basket as well."

"Oh," said Cubby.

"It would be nice if you had a fish basket," said Mrs. Pelican. "You eat a good many fish, but every time you catch one you have to stop and eat it right away. Now, when I catch a fish I just drop it down into my basket, and then I can eat it when I get hungry or carry it home to the family."

"That certainly is convenient," said Mommie Bear. "But I didn't expect to see you here. Although I'm really not at all surprised."

"I've been coming for a good many years," said Mrs. Pelican. "I say if Yellowstone Park is a good place for people and bears and gulls, it's a good place for pelicans too. I'm still a bit shy. I keep a good bit to myself. We pelicans live out in the lake on an island—it's so safe there. I like to be safe."

"I feel that way too," said Mommie Bear, "although a lot of my relations seem to have made themselves very much at home here. This is my first trip through the Park and I still feel a little timid. But, Cubby, here, gets acquainted with everything and everyone and is having such a good time. We are on our way to the next place. Can you tell us what we shall see?"

Mrs. Gull looked at Mrs. Pelican and Mrs. Pelican looked at Mrs. Gull. "Well, really," said Mrs. Gull, "I can't. You see, we fly everywhere we go. It's a wonderful way to travel."

"If you follow the road," said Mrs. Pelican, "you'll come to the Lake Hotel and the Fish Hatcheries."

"Then we will go there," said Mommie Bear.

"It's always a puzzle to me, about those hatcheries," Mrs. Gull told them. "I've peeped into the windows and there are long tanks of water just filled with fish eggs. These eggs hatch into minnows. The minnows grow into fish. Now, the idea of fish hatching from eggs always bothers me. They haven't a n y feathers, so why should they hatch from eggs? Can you tell me that?"

Mrs. Gull

"There are a great many strange things in the world," said Mrs. Pelican wisely. "But Mother Fish is very careless with her eggs. Usually she just leaves them in the water without any nest. It's a wonder any of them hatch. Now, you and I, Mrs. Gull, would never think of doing such a thing."

"Indeed we would not. But there are some mothers of the fish family who guard their eggs," answered Mrs. Gull. "It is fortunate for us that most of them do not."

"I'd love to see the Fish Hatchery," said Cubby,

clasping his little furry paws. "Do you suppose we can, Mommie?"

"And there is a wonderful hotel there," added Mrs. Pelican. "You know, a hotel is where the people stay when they are not riding around. Farther on is what they call a lodge, with a big house and lots of little cabins. Some of the people live in the big house, some in the cabins, and some of them live in tents that they carry about with them. It is very interesting."

"We are going to see it," said Mommie Bear. "Thanks for telling us so much about it. Come on, Cubby, dear, if we are going to see Yellowstone Park, we must keep moving."

CHAPTER VIII

MASTER MEDDLESOME

IT was lovely walking along the narrow edge of the lake with the mountains rising up all around it. Cubby and his mother had to stop and admire all the pretty things as they passed. They were really sorry for the people who had to drive so fast in their cars.

"I'm sure they miss a great deal," said Cubby.

At last they came in sight of a large building. "It's the Fish Hatchery," said Cubby, gleefully. And it was. "I wonder if we can go in. Look, Mommie. Do you see any sign with *'no bears admitted'* printed on it?"

"There are a good many signs," said Mommie Bear, "but I don't see anything on them about bears. I don't think I would like to go in there, Cubby. I'm not used to houses."

But just then there was such a commotion! Out of the door came galloping a half-grown cub bear. Behind him was a man. "Get out," he shouted, "you meddlesome cub!" His voice sounded as if he meant it. And the young bear was getting out just as fast as he could. Cubby and his mother saw that he was running right to the spot where they were hidden in the bushes.

He stopped quickly when he saw them there and looked from one to the other. "Why, how do you do?" he

48

said. And then he grinned. "Did you see that man chase me out of the hatchery? Well, there are glass cases in there filled with the best-looking fish you ever saw. It looked like a real meal to me. You know, glass is something you can see through just as though it weren't there. I was about to grab one of the fish but I upset the case and it broke, and well, there was quite a mess. The man yelled and I ran, so I didn't get even a fish."

"I'm glad we didn't go in," said Mommie Bear. "We might have gotten into trouble. What is your name, young man?"

"I guess it's Meddlesome," said the young bear sheepishly. "Mother says it is, and she says I'll get into

"Here come three bears!"

trouble if I don't change my ways. It seems as if everything I do is the wrong thing. Let's go on up to the
hotel and see what we can see." So the three bears went
on together.

"It is a large den," said Mommie Bear. "In all my
life I never have seen such a den."

"Oh, look," called a voice, "here come the three bears!
The great, huge bear and the middle-size bear, and the
tiny little bear." The three bears looked and they saw a
little girl with long golden curls. Cubby sat down and
folded his little paws. He thought she was the prettiest
person he had ever seen. Mommie Bear sat down and
smiled her nicest smile. "They look just as if they had
come out of a storybook," said the little girl, gleefully.
"If only they had a little house and little beds and little
bowls, and the little chairs, we could play that I was
Goldilocks."

"Let's take a picture of them," said the little girl's
mother. "The big bear and the little bear are sitting so
still. If the middle-size bear just sits down, it will be
lovely."

Mommie Bear looked at the black box with one eye,
but this time she kept very still. These people seemed
kind; perhaps it wouldn't hurt if they did "take" something.

"I'll throw them something to eat," said the little
girl's daddy, "and that may interest them."

But Meddlesome would not be quiet. He wanted to
see the thing that took the picture. He wanted to

do everything that he should not do. So, at last, the little girl's daddy and mother took the little girl away into the hotel.

"Oh," said Cubby, "you spoiled it all, Meddlesome. Why wouldn't you sit down and be still? Now the little Goldilocks is gone."

Meddlesome sighed. "I am always doing the wrong thing," he said, sadly. "I'm always sorry afterward."

And it was always so. Meddlesome could be depended upon to do what he should not. He meddled with cars that stood by the hotel. He meddled with tents that people had made up nicely for their night's sleep.

"I think," said Mommie Bear, "that we will be going on. Meddlesome is bad company. If we stay with him, we shall get into trouble too." So they went on together through the moonlight. They looked back at the hotel with all the lights in its windows, and Cubby sighed a happy little cubby sigh.

"It's nice to sleep under the stars," he said, as he cuddled down close to his mother for the night.

CHAPTER IX

THE ELF IN DRAGON MOUTH SPRING

"I WISH we had one of those books," said Cubby as he watched a carload of people go by. "There must be very interesting things in them. It seems queer to see people riding along reading out of a book instead of looking at all the pretty things about them."

"My dear son," answered Mommie Bear, "that is a guidebook. It tells them what they are to see ahead, so they can watch, and not miss anything. It would be fine if there were a guidebook for bears. The best we can do is to ask, as we go along, and learn from our relations who live here and know all about it."

"Of course we have all summer," said Cubby.

"I asked a wise old bear about what we were to see to-day," said Mommie Bear, "and I can promise you, Cubby, that we are to have a very wonderful time. So keep your eyes open."

Mommie Bear and Cubby moved quietly along near the edge of the road. The sun was warm on their backs now, for the hot days had come. To be sure, it grew quite cool at night and all the cub babies were glad for their warm fur coats. Often cars stopped. Kindly people gave the dear little cub a choice bit from their lunch boxes.

Sometimes they took pictures of Cubby and his mother before they drove away. Mommie Bear didn't mind now, although she did wonder what it was all about. They found some more of the Paint Pots, or "fairy houses," as Cubby liked to call them. And along the hillside was the Dragon Mouth Spring. They knew that was its name, for they heard people reading about it from their books.

"I will tell a story about this," said Mommie Bear. "You told such a pretty one last time, Cubby."

"Once upon a time there was a Naughty Elf. He was always making trouble. He liked to tease everyone. So the other elves planned what they would do to him. 'We will laugh,' they said. 'When he teases us, we will just laugh and pay no attention to him.' So they did. Now, this made the Naughty Elf very angry. And the more he thought about it the more angry he became. He grew to be very disagreeable. The good little elves were frightened. They went to the Good Fairy and asked her to help them.

" 'I will,' said the Good Fairy. 'I will give him a cave to live in all by himself where he can be as unhappy as he wishes without making others unhappy.' So she took the Naughty Elf and put him into a little cave by himself.

" 'I do not want to stay here,' said the Naughty Elf.

" 'You must stay here,' said the Good Fairy, 'until you can be kind and good. Now you only make everyone who comes near you unhappy.'

"And so the Naughty Elf sits in there by himself.

Every once in awhile he comes rushing to the door. And then he remembers, he must stay there until he can be good and kind. So he goes back more angry than ever. People say a dragon lives in the cave and they call it the Dragon Mouth Spring. They do not know it is just a Naughty Elf who will not try to be kind."

"I am sorry for him," said Cubby. "It must be very uncomfortable to be in such a temper. I think being angry all the time would be worse than being sick all the time."

"Oh, much worse," said Mommie Bear. "I believe one might feel very sick and still be happy, but one could never be angry and happy at the same time, never!"

"When I feel like getting angry, I will remember the poor little Naughty Elf," said Cubby as they started on their journey again. "I know it is just a story, Mommie Bear, but when the water came puffing and steaming to the mouth of the cave, I could almost believe that it was our Naughty Elf in a rage; and then when he ran back, I could almost hear him sobbing to himself. I'm sure that some day he will learn his lesson and be a good, kind Elf and come out into the sun and be happy. Then, maybe, he can go through Yellowstone Park just as we are doing."

"He will be happy then," said Mommie Bear. "Let us now go into the forest and see if we can find something nice for our dinner. You must always know how to find your food. We may not always live in the Park where people give us so much to eat. And, really, I am hungry for a few nice grubs; the people never give us any."

It was while she was showing Cubby how to overturn fallen logs for choice insects and how to choose just what

She was showing Cubby how to overturn fallen logs

he should eat that they heard a friendly voice, and looking up saw their old friend Mr. Moose. But how he had changed! Such strange things were growing out of his head!

"I'm growing some new ones," he told them. "It won't be long, and I believe this pair will be the nicest I have had. At first they are all covered with a sort of down and I say my horns are 'in the velvet.' But I scratch the velvet off on trees and they grow hard and strong until I have a splendid new pair. Just now I'm keeping to myself; I always feel rather undressed without my antlers. Are you going to the falls?"

"How far is it?" asked Mommie Bear.

"Just a few miles on. The falls are very beautiful. They treat the bears very well there too, I am told. In fact, I understand they feed them regularly."

"We have been fed a good bit already," said Mommie Bear, "but we will go along and see. We do not want to miss anything. I suppose the next time we see you, Mr. Moose, you will have your fine new horns. Come, Cubby, dear."

CHAPTER X

THE WATER SPRITE OF THE YELLOW-STONE

THROUGH a lovely path Cubby and his mother found their way to the great falls.

Long before they got there they were thrilled with the sound that came to their ears, for the water sang a song of joy as it leaped through the air down, down, down, t h r e e hundred and eight feet to the canyon below.

"It sounds like a very wild, great creature," said Cubby, hurrying ahead. "Do tell me how a river can make such a loud noise."

"You shall see," said his mother.

But when they came

The Great Falls

to where they could see, Cubby could only sit and look and look. For a long time he did not speak. He wanted only to watch that great flood of water from the pine-clad hills take its grand leap downward. He loved to watch the spray that rose as the water leaped and bounded. At last they found their way to a spot where they could look down upon the great fall and see the beauty of the canyon below.

"I will tell you a story," said Mommie Bear, dreamily. "Once upon a time there was a lovely Water Sprite. She lived in the great Lake Yellowstone. It was very quiet in the great lake and the lovely creature sometimes wished that she might go out into the world and see all the beautiful things that lay beyond the banks of her home.

"Her friends begged her not to go. 'You would be lost,' they told her. 'Stay with us and be happy. Dear Water Sprite, this home is safe.'

"But the lovely Water Sprite said: 'I am of no use here. I would like to go out into the world. I would like to find a way to make people happy.'

" 'You cannot make people happy,' they told her. 'What would you do? You would only lose yourself in the mountains.' But when her friends saw that she was unhappy, they said: 'Very well, you shall go. You shall go out in the world, but you never will find your way back.'

" 'I will not be sorry,' she told them, 'if I can find a way to bring any beauty or happiness into the world.

Who would wish to lie idly in the sun if he could do anything to make the world better or more beautiful?'

"Her friends told her good-by sadly and she set out upon her great adventure. She traveled along smooth paths for a time, but at last she found a wonderful place, where the soils were different. 'I will make something beautiful here,' she cried; 'I will make a canyon—a gorgeous, beautiful canyon that everyone will love and that people will come from afar to see.'

"All nature helped her. The frosts and the winds and the rains and the snows. Deeper and deeper she carved her canyon—down, down, down, down, a straight wall with here and there great lovely spires, carved and made beautiful. And the fairies that live in the ground peeped out to see the beauty that the Water Sprite had made. They let the heat and steam from their houses rise up through the cracks and crevices, and a wonderful thing happened. The most gorgeous colors came out upon the canyon walls so beautifully made. Here was the deepest orange fading into the purest lemon. There was bright crimson, shading to brick color and trailing off into a glorious pink. And there was black, coal-black, and ivory white.

"'We will creep down,' said the pine trees, 'and make our glowing green a bright spot of color too upon the canyon walls.'

"So the mosses and the cedars crept down because they loved to live in such a fairyland of color. The blue of the sky arched overhead.

" 'It is beautiful,' said the Water Sprite, 'more beautiful than ever I had dared to hope. I wonder if there is anything more beautiful in all the world. How grateful I am to all who have helped me!'

"But she kept solid the wall that entered the canyon, for most of all she loved that wonderful leap that the water made down, down, down into the fairyland of color. And so the Water Sprite had made something very beautiful for the world to see—a lovely canyon, not so large as some others, but one that for beauty of form and brilliancy of color is not excelled."

"And people and bears," said Cubby, happily, "come and look at its beauty and are not able to think of words that can tell how it makes them feel."

"It makes me feel very, very small," said Mommie Bear.

"It makes me feel happy," said Cubby. "Happy that I live in such a beautiful, beautiful world."

Cubby and his mother watched the people as they came and went. Strange, but few of them noticed the mother bear and her little cub as they stood and looked down at the water as it plunged into the canyon dripping with color. Some of them said, "Beautiful," over and over. And some of them said "Gorgeous," and "Wonderful." But none of them seemed to find a word that just suited. Cubby listened for one. He wanted to find just the word to use when he looked down into the beautiful Yellowstone Canyon. But he did not find it. He liked best the people who stood and looked in silence just as if, Cubby thought, they were making a picture in their minds that they could carry away with them.

And so Cubby sat on the edge of the canyon wall and looked and looked and tried to make a picture in his mind, a picture that he could still see even when he shut his eyes. For he wanted to be able to think of the canyon always, even if there were no word that could describe its beauty to others.

CHAPTER XI

CANYON DAYS

CUBBY and his mother decided to spend some time around the canyon. The hotel was very lovely, the people very friendly and kind. It was fun going about. Over the canyon edge on the high carved rock formations, safe from harm, were nests of the osprey, great birds that caught fish and carried them to their babies. It was interesting to watch the father bird come with his cry of greeting and then to see the parents feed the well-behaved babies. During the day the mother bird hovered over the nest to shield her babies from the hot rays of the sun. The people liked to watch them too.

At certain hours each day the bears were given a great feast. Cubby and Mommie Bear thought they had never

The Osprey

been treated so well in all their lives. A great load of food was brought from the hotel and all the bears from the woods around seemed to know just what time the banquet would be ready.

And they came—brown bears and black bears, big bears and middle-sized bears, good-natured bears and cranky bears. They were all ready to take part in the feast.

But there were others who came—lots of others. They did not come to eat. They came to watch. They were people. Fat people and thin people, big people, little people and middle-size people, young people and old people, black, white, red and yellow people—all kinds of people.

Sometimes Cubby would stop eating and look at them. He wondered what they were thinking. They did not say "Beautiful," or "Gorgeous," but they laughed a great deal and seemed to be having a good time.

When a mother bear cuffed her young son or daughter for being greedy, the people seemed to think it was the greatest joke. They even laughed when two great bears that wanted to eat in the same corner made deep rumbling growls—although they edged a bit farther away.

"They think we are queer," a nice old bear told Cubby. "They are only used to bears in cages, so they find us very interesting. No matter how often we eat, there are always people who like to watch us."

"I am not used to them," said Cubby, uneasily.

"There are so many of them. Before I came to the Park I had not seen any of them, not even in a cage!"

The good-natured old bear had to stop and laugh. "That is a good joke," he chuckled. "How queer they would feel if they knew that we think they are as funny as they think we are!"

"Wait a minute," said Cubby; "say that again—I couldn't quite understand it. But I do think they are funny. Are they never in cages?"

"No, indeed, not that I have ever heard of anyway. Sometimes they have a bear in a cage. They teach him tricks. Long ago there was an old bear who said that he had escaped from a circus and he told us many strange things about people. I really could hardly believe all he had to say."

"I think we will spend several days here," said Mommie Bear. "I don't know when I have been in such a pleasant place—wonderful scenery and lots of company."

"You should go to the hotel to-night," said the friendly bear. "They have jolly times there and at the lodges. People like good times."

"Look, Mommie," cried Cubby, "there is our friend." And sure enough, there stood one of the Rangers.

"Oh, he is always here," said the good-natured bear. "He is our friend too. He always comes down when we eat and sees that no harm comes to us. We were talking about him the other day. Someone said that if a man should try to take one of our cubs the Ranger wouldn't let him. We know that as long as he stands there everything will be all right. This is a very safe and happy place for bears and people."

"Come, Cubby," said Mommie Bear, "let us be moving. We will go up by the hotel. It is better to leave before all the food is gone, for some ill-natured bear may get cross over it. We are going to see all we can of these people to-night."

And they did. There was music and the people danced. Cubby and his mother stood up on their hind legs and peeped into a window.

"How different they look!" said Cubby. "See that lady, Mommie! To-day she wore heavy leather boots and a brown suit—but look at her now!"

"She looks like a fairy," said Mommie Bear, wistfully. "That dress she has on might be made of the silver spray at the falls with the colors of the sunset sewed into it. Yes, sonny, people seem to be able to change their clothes as bears never, never can."

"I am sorry," said Cubby, "that you can never have a lovely new dress, Mommie, but you are very beautiful to me. I wouldn't know you in anything like that. You would be very strange and different. I should be frightened."

Mommie Bear drew little Cubby close in her arms. "Then we will not wish for such things," she said.

"Boom, boom," said the drum, "Ta-ta-ta," sang the piano, "Hummmmmmmm, hummmmmmmm," sighed the violin.

"We will dance," said Mommie Bear. So she took hold of Cubby's furry little brown paw and they danced together. "Bears dance this way, and bears dance that way," sang Mommie Bear, "oh, ho, oh, ho! Form your hands in a ring; then you do the big bear fling, oh, ho, oh, ho." It ended in a back summersault and Cubby came up begging for more. But Mommie thought they should see more instead.

Not all of the people were at the dance. Some of them were listening to a very wise lecture being given by one of the Rangers. Others were getting ready for bed. Little columns of smoke rose from dying camp fires. Sleepy babies said in sleepy-baby fashion that they did not want to go to bed.

Mommie Bear and Cubby sat and listened. There were good smells in the air. Cubby's keen little nose told him all about them. Bit by bit the camp grew quiet. Cubby cuddled down beside his mother and closed his eyes. It had been a long day and he was tired.

He tried to see the beautiful canyon. He thought of the Water Sprite. Perhaps she looked like the lovely lady that he had just seen. Yes, there she was. He could see her now. She was dressed in a long trailing gown, silver mist, flecked with gold and crimson and silver. She was so beautiful, and now—she was at the top of the canyon wall, and now she was floating down, down, d—o—w—n! and she was singing. Her voice was soft and sweet. Cubby slept.

CHAPTER XII

CUBS AND TOURISTS IN CAMP

CUBBY awoke with a start. He did not know whether it was the sudden movement of his mother that had roused him or the strange noise in the air. Whatever it was, he found himself on his feet beside Mommie Bear. The noise hurt his ears. It was sharp and ringing. And then he heard voices.

"Get out!" cried out someone from a tent near by. And then there was a noise again. It clanged and jangled. Mother Bear dropped down on her haunches and began to chuckle. But Cubby did not know what she could be chuckling about.

Then from the tent there darted a small black shape—a mischievous young cub. Behind it followed someone very strangely dressed. Cubby

"Get out!" cried someone

67

rubbed his eyes and looked again. People were queer. He had never seen one dressed like that. A suit of white—all white. Yes, and there was someone else with a long dress of white, clear to the ground. It was odd! And the noise! It came from something they had in their hands. Dear me, it was a tin pan, and they pounded it with a spoon! No wonder it made a noise loud enough to frighten a bear half out of his wits. The little bear was still running and Mommie Bear still chuckling. And, strange to say, the people were laughing too.

Others in tents near by stuck out their heads and one called, "Well, did you trap a bear?"

"I told you not to keep any bacon in your tent," called another.

"I believe you," called the man in the white suit, "and here goes the bacon and the bears are welcome to it. Just so they keep out of our tent." He tossed something that he held in his hand. It was wrapped in brown paper and it fell right at Mommie Bear's feet.

Cubby sniffed. It was the most wonderful odor he had ever smelled. Mommie Bear chuckled again. "Meddlesome!" she said, softly. "Cubby, that was Meddlesome. Well, we will eat the bacon. After all, it is only our reward for being good bears and not bothering people. I hope that you will never be like that naughty rascal. Some day he will get into real trouble. Here, sonny, take this." Cubby ate it up quicker than a wink. And then he sat and thought about how good it had tasted and wished he had not gobbled it down so quickly. Mmmmmmmmm, it was perfectly delicious!

Everything was quiet now. The people had all gone back to sleep. Quite early Cubby and Mommie Bear set out for the woods to find their breakfast. And here they found Meddlesome digging for grubs.

"No," he said, "I haven't bothered looking at the canyon. It is too much fun getting things from the tourists."

"You will get into trouble," said Mommie Bear, wisely. "Did your mother not teach you better?"

"Where are you from?" asked Meddlesome. "My mother is a Park bear. She is clever. She taught me how to beg from the tourists. But I ran away and left her. Anyway, I'm big enough now to get along by myself."

"You mean," said Mommie Bear, "that your mother taught you to beg? I can't believe it."

"Well, she did. Early in the spring she took me to a narrow road where the people had to pass. I would run out into the road and wait for the cars and they could not pass until they gave me something. The people called it a 'holdup,' but they didn't mind, and I'm sure I didn't."

"How shocking!" said Mommie Bear; "I think you were very ill-mannered."

But Meddlesome only laughed. "I found a car this morning," he said; "there was no one there so I climbed in."

"You climbed into a car!" Mommie Bear could hardly believe her ears. "What would you have done if it had started to run away?"

"I never thought of that. I threw out a lot of stuff—pillows and things. One pillow—well, it broke, and the strangest things came out of it. I was frightened and I hit it with my paw. The air was filled with flying things that got into my nose and choked me. I never saw anything like it. And the more I hit it the worse the things flew. I jumped out and ran away but I haven't gotten rid of the stuff yet. See, it is still on my fur coat."

"Feathers!" said Mommie Bear. "Just soft, downy feathers."

Meddlesome looked again. "Feathers," he said, "now look at that; there might have been a bird or something good in that bag. Oh, dear, think what I've missed!"

"Come, Cubby, dear," said Mommie Bear, "we will be moving on." As soon as they were hidden in the bushes she looked down anxiously at her baby bear. "Promise me, Cubby," she said with a queer little choke in her voice, "that you will never be like Meddlesome."

Cubby laid his furry brown head against her. "Of course not, Mommie, dear," he laughed. "Poor Meddlesome didn't have a mother like mine. He doesn't know any better."

"That's right," said Mommie Bear. "Poor Meddlesome doesn't know any better so he isn't to blame for his naughty ways. I'll not worry any more, Cubby. I know

I can trust you to remember to be honest and kind. But look, there are some people. I guess they own the car that Meddlesome climbed into. Just see all the feathers! We will not go this way. They might think we were to blame for it and make trouble for us. I don't blame them for being provoked at naughty Meddlesome, but after this I guess they will lock their car."

CHAPTER XIII

LESSONS AT MOUNT WASHBURN

"IT is time," said Mommie Bear, "that you learned to do many things. How sad it would be if I should neglect to teach you how to live and be safe and happy, all because I was too interested in looking at the scenery!"

"But I have learned," said Cubby, in surprise. "I have been learning all the time. I'll show you some of the things I can do. I can climb a tree just as well as any bear. See me, Mommie?" Mommie Bear saw him and she nodded her head in approval.

"Very good, sonny, and if danger is ever near, you climb the nearest tree and let me look after the trouble. Now, now, Cubby, listen to me! There will be plenty of time for you to look after troubles when you are grown. Just watch me and see how I manage them. Now tell me, what is the best food to eat early in the spring, just as soon as you can get it?"

"Grass," said Cubby.

"Grass," repeated Mommie Bear. "Eat lots of grass. It will make you grow fine and strong and keep you from being sick. No matter how much else you may find, no matter how many nice grubs, or berries or sweets, don't forget grass. Always eat a lot just before you go to bed in the fall. I'll remind you this fall, but next fall you will have to remember for yourself."

"Why, Mommie?"

"Because then you will be large enough to go out in the world and seek your fortune. Bears like to be alone. They like to look at things by themselves and live by themselves. Of course they don't mind a little visit now and then with other bears, but you will find that you will get along better if you keep by yourself. I don't care for anyone but my little cubs. Of course I love them. But I wouldn't want to live with a lot of bears or go in a herd as the elk do."

And so, day by day, Mommie Bear told Cubby more and more about the world he lived in and how he should

"I can climb a tree"

live in it. And day by day they moved along up the canyon until they came to a trail that turned toward a mountaintop.

"Shall we go?" asked Mommie Bear. "It would be lovely to be on a mountain again, Cubby."

"Let's," said Cubby.

But the trail they followed was one made by the bears

that lived on the mountain. Sometimes Cubby and his mother almost forgot that anyone else lived there. The country was so rough and wild, with great armies of pines marching up the mountainsides. And flowers! The glowing rose of the fireweed made bright spots of color on open patches, vivid against the green of the background pine.

Mommie Bear showed Cubby the different flowers. He had already seen the clematis in bloom. At first he thought it looked like a white snowbank as the masses of small white flowers almost covered the green of the leaves and the branches of the vine. He had watched for the evening primrose that loved best to bloom in the coolness of the night and that went to sleep during the hot, sunny hours. The blue of the larkspur like a bit of deep-blue sky always interested him. There were so many lovely flowers upon the mountainsides—lupines, the red orange of the paint brush, the flat white heads of the wild parsnip!

"They are pretty, but they are not to eat, are they, Mommie Bear?" Cubby asked.

"They will go to seed and we will like the seeds," said his mother. "The insects like the flowers and we like the insects, so, after all, they are useful to us.

"But let us learn some more about our food, Cubby. There are lots of nice insects here. And it is a good thing too. People sometimes don't like them, I am told, but if it were not for the insects there would not be so many, many lovely flowers. The insects carry the flower

dust from blossom to blossom, and that is what makes
them grow."

"The birds like insects too," said Cubby. "I've noticed
that myself."

"You are right, sonny; the birds like them very much,
and there would not be birds here if they could not find
food. Even the fish in the water like them. There would
not be so many birds or fish either if there were no insects.
So let us be thankful for insects, sonny. Every one
should be thankful for them.

"And the ants! Oh, they are delicious! These big
black timber ants nest in old hollow logs. I always stop
and look at a fallen log like this one. It is apt to have
a big colony of ants under it. Here is another kind.
These are called the termites, or white ants. It's queer,
for they are not really white or really ants, either. It's
funny how different they are in size. Some of them have
broad heads—they seem to be the workers. Some of
them have long heads, and they are the fighters. And
these big ones—look—they are ten times as long as the
others—they are the queens. I have often wished that I
could watch them longer, but I always get so hungry I
just eat them up before I learn all I'd like to about
them." Mommie Bear laughed. "I guess," she said,
"it's more bearlike to eat them than it is to watch them."

"Tell me about the butterflies," said Cubby. "It must
be fun to fly about as they do. I often watch them."

"Oh, there are lots of lovely ones here," said Mommie
Bear. "See that yellow one with the black edges on his

wings! You can find him almost anywhere. That little brown one too, I've seen him in many places. There is one kind that you see only on the mountaintops. It's strange, but butterflies seem to have places that they like just as do other things. Look, there is a pretty little blue fellow and there is a big red one that likes the milkweed blossoms. I'll show you, too, the little painted lady when we see her. She lives around the thistle blossoms. You'll know her by the pink spots on her wings."

"It seems to me," said Cubby, a bit wistfully, "as if Mother Nature had put all her pretty colors on the butterflies."

"Don't be envious, sonny; you would never want to be a butterfly even though they can fly and are pretty. At first they are worms and then they make a house for themselves and go to sleep. When they waken they have wings and are butterflies. Most of them are gone with the first frost; their lives are short, so they should be bright and pretty to make up. They are of many colors and they fly in the sun. Did I ever tell you about their relations that fly at night?"

"Oh, no, but tell me now, Mommie," begged Cubby.

"They are much like the butterflies in every way but they are night fliers and so they are called moths. There is one kind that loves the sage brush. It's strange, isn't it, that moths should like the darkness when their cousins like the day? Now we must be moving. I'll show you how to find the best insect food for bears."

CHAPTER XIV

THE BEAR THAT LIVED IN A HOUSE

AT last Cubby and his mother reached Tower Falls. Already buses and cars loaded with people were coming in, some to stay for the night, others to go on to the next lodge.

"I think we will stay," said Mommie Bear. "I'd like to inquire about the country and what we shall see after we leave here."

"I wonder where all those people are going," said Cubby. "Shall we go with them?"

"Let us wait," said his mother. "Look, over yonder by that house are a lot of people. Can you see what they are looking at, Cubby?"

"Why," said Cubby, "it's a bear"—his voice was filled with surprise—"and it's looking out of the basement window of that house. Isn't that funny? Did you ever see a bear in a house before?"

"Well, I do declare," said Mommie Bear. "It is really, and what a big, fat, sleek creature he is! But, then, I'm not at all surprised. One can see almost anything in Yellowstone Park. He seems to be having a nice time. Perhaps it may be pleasant living in a house after one gets used to it. After the people go away we will talk to him and ask him about it."

"I would like to go now," said Cubby, impatiently. "I would like to have them look at me."

Mommie Bear looked at Cubby in surprise. She shook her great head. "Cubby, you frighten me," she said. "I almost wish that I had not brought you to the Park. You are growing so bold. Never push yourself forward, son. But then," she thought to herself, "times have changed. When I was a cub, I had never seen a man, and I would have been frightened to death to be so near one. If you should go now, Cubby, the people might turn to you, for you are still a baby. Do you suppose the big black bear would like that? Indeed he would not. I am afraid it would make him very angry and we do not want any trouble with our relations. So let us wait until the people have moved away."

So they sat and waited. At last the crowd moved on. The great bear crawled out of his window. He looked about. Near by was a drinking fountain, with a trough half full of water. Lazily he crawled into the water and lay down comfortably for a few minutes.

Mommie Bear and Cubby drew nearer. "How do you do?" said Mommie Bear.

The great, sleek black bear raised his head sleepily. "Why, how do you do?" he said, lazily.

"My little son and I have been watching you," said Mommie Bear. "Do you live here?"

"Do *I* live here?" said he. "Do you mean to say you have not heard of me?" His voice showed his surprise.

"No, I haven't," said Mommie Bear a bit snappishly.

"Well, where have you been?" asked the great, sleek black bear. "I supposed everyone had heard of the bear that lives in the house that Jack built," he repeated with emphasis. And when Mommie Bear did not answer he raised his head quickly with a great splashing of water. "Why don't you say something? Everyone says, 'Oh, look, there is a bear that lives in a house!' Aren't you surprised?"

Mommie Bear shook her head. "I'm not surprised at anything," she said, and her tone was not exactly pleasant. "Imagine a great, sleek black bear like you living in a house! But then I suppose there are other bears doing that here."

Tower Falls

The bear crawled out from his tub. He was provoked. "Listen," he said, "I made up a verse about myself. I'll tell it to you and then, maybe, you will appreciate me. I have lots of time, so I make up verses."

"Well, go on," said Mommie Bear, "I never heard any verses. But," and she hesitated, "I wouldn't want Cubby to hear anything that wasn't nice."

"It's very nice," said the sleek black bear; "you see, it's about me."

"Well, I'm not so sure," said Mommie Bear. "But go on. If we don't like it, we shall not stay."

The great bear arose on his haunches and folded his paws under his chin. "I'll tell it to you," he said, "and you should feel complimented. No person in all the world has ever heard it. And if I were to tell it to them, they wouldn't understand, for they cannot speak our language. Are you ready?"

"Quite ready," said Mommie Bear.

"All right—here it is:
> "I'm a civilized bear,
>   Black, and sleek, and fair—
>   Dum, diddle, dum diddle dum dee—
>   I live in a house as snug as a mouse.
>   And the people all love me.
> I'm a civilized bear,
> For ants I do not care—
>   Dum, diddle, dum diddle dum dee—
> They feed me right
> From morn till night,

For the people all love me.
I'm a civilized bear
Without ever a care—
    Dum, diddle, dum diddle dum dee—
As I said before,
I'm not wild any more,
    The people are wild about me!''

He sat for a moment with his eyes closed. And then he opened them. "Why don't you say something?" he asked. "Like 'Beautiful!' or 'Isn't he sweet!' ?"

"Well," said Mommie Bear, "I—I guess I was afraid to speak my thoughts. And I think Cubby and I had better be moving on. It isn't always wise to say just what one thinks. Come, Cubby."

They did not turn back but went on over the hill. But there stood the great, sleek black bear looking after them in surprise. Then he shook his head. "Some bears are so ignorant," he sighed.

And so he crawled back through his window into his basement.

CHAPTER XV

TRIPS FROM TOWER FALLS

"THERE are a lot of interesting things around here," said Mr. Brown Bear. "The Falls, the 'Tower Falls,' you know, are just as pretty as can be. Not so high as the Falls back at the canyon, but there's a drop of 132 feet, just a straight ribbon of water."

"They must be pretty," said Mommie Bear. "What else is there to see?"

"Well, you really should go over and see the buffalo. There is a herd of a thousand over in the mountains. Have you ever seen one?"

"I've seen a moose," said Cubby.

But Mr. Brown Bear shook his head. "They're different," he said, "a lot different."

"I've heard of them," said Mommie Bear. "I remember being told that there used to be hundreds of them in the country but that there are not so many any more."

"You're right," nodded Mr. Brown Bear. "There are a few over at the next big camping place, but I would rather see them out in the mountains. They act more natural. Very few people take the trouble to see the big herd."

"We will," said Mommie Bear. "I'd like to see them running around being happy like we are."

"Better watch out, they're rather easily provoked," said Mr. Brown Bear, "but, then, you know how to take care of yourselves."

"We'll not bother them," said Mommie Bear. "We are not looking for trouble."

So Cubby and his mother set out to see the buffalo. They chose their own way rather than following a trail.

"I am happy," said Cubby; "the world is so filled with beauty. I wish I were a bird and could sing."

"I feel like singing too," said his mother. "But, look, we will have to cross this long bridge."

"I'm not afraid," said Cubby, "and see, beyond is a new kind of country. Are those buffalo, Mommie Bear?"

"No, Cubby," laughed Mommie Bear, "they are great bowlders. How strange that this grassy flat should be strewn with these huge rounded stones!"

"It looks as though some great giant had been playing with them," laughed Cubby, "and had tossed them here and there over the valley. One could have a jolly time playing hide-and-seek here, couldn't he?"

"I have heard," said Mommie Bear wisely, "that once a great river of ice swept down these canyons. It carried great stones and bowlders with it. When at last it melted of course the bowlders were left."

"Then the river of ice would be the giant," said Cubby.

"Why, so it would," said Mommie Bear.

"The great giant lived high up on the mountain,"

said Cubby. "He liked to gather bowlders and would pull them out of great cliffs or from hollows or wherever he passed. He held them fast in his arms. Inch by inch he moved down the mountainside. The days grew warmer—the great giant found that he had more stones than he could well carry, but he pushed on and on with them.

" 'I will carry them to the sea,' he said. But he grew more tired each day and his load more heavy, until at last he laid them down and ran away without them. And here they are yet!"

"And here are a lot more of them," said Mommie Bear. "Look, Cubby, in this canyon they lie in heaps! They will be here for a long, long time, I feel sure. Only some great giant strength will move them. But now we must keep on. We have to go up this canyon and turn north. That is the way to the buffalo ranch."

Cubby saw them first, but for some time his mother had known they were not far away. Her keen sense of smell had told her.

"Why, look," said Cubby, "he's big. Ooooh, he's as big as Mr. Moose!"

"Hush," said Mommie Bear. "Listen, Cubby, there is something very near us." Through the bushes a friendly bear thrust its head.

"Oh," said Mommie Bear in a relieved voice, "I'm so glad to see you. We're going through the Park for the first time and there is so much we do not understand.

We came to see the bison, or buffalo, as they are called, and we wish we knew someone who could tell us all about them."

"Well," said the newcomer, "I guess I'm just the one who can do that. You say you are new here? Then I guess you are not as bold as some of our folks that we see down around the lodges."

"We are," said Mommie Bear, "and we are not."

The other bear laughed. "Then I like you," he said. "I live out here and am happier than all those bears that stay around the camps. I know lots about the buffalo and I'll be glad to tell you. They are shy creatures and are easily provoked. Now, that big one yonder is about six feet high and ten feet long. He's strong. I've seen him

"I know lots about the buffalo"

knock down trees. Look at his big head. When he puts it down and charges at anything you do not want to be in the way."

"His head looks so heavy," said Cubby, "one would 'most think he would get tired carrying it around. And isn't that a funny great hump behind his neck. Can he run very fast?"

"Few animals can outstrip him," said their new friend. "When traveling over rough ground he can scarcely be beaten. Long years ago there were hundreds of thousands of them in the land, but now there are not many left."

"What has happened to them?" asked Cubby.

"They have been hunted by man for their beautiful heavy fur coats. His coat is so warm that he never feels the cold."

"How wonderful!" said Mommie Bear. "I am glad that they are safe here and can be happy. Do they live very long, do you know?"

"Oh, they have quite a long life. I have been told some of them are almost forty years old. But look, that great one yonder sees us. There he goes! Watch him run!"

Cubby watched the great beast lower his monstrous head and move forward. Then, breaking into a gallop, with head held low and hoofs rising higher than his head, he disappeared in the thickets beyond. Now they could not see him but they heard him crashing through the underbrush.

"I'm glad he didn't run this way," said Cubby, trembling a little.

"We have seen something very worth while," nodded Mommie Bear, "something few of the people see, I believe."

"Yes," said their friend. "You have. The people who go through our parks do not see much of the wild life. Very few animals except bears come out to the roadside or to the camps. If people had time to follow the trails, they would find many, many interesting things that they will never see otherwise."

"I am glad," said Cubby, "that we have time."

"But even our time is going fast," said Mommie Bear. "I am afraid that we will not be able to see all the lovely things in the Park."

"Then you will have to spend another summer here," said the bear. "I have spent all my life here and still find many things that are new and beautiful to me. If you go on from here, you will see some of the most wonderful scenery in the Park."

"I plan to go back to Tower Falls now," said Mommie Bear, "but maybe we shall visit the Park again. Perhaps next year."

"Well, good-by," said their friend; "I'll be looking for you next summer."

"Thanks for telling us about the buffalo," said Cubby.

"Oh, you are welcome, it was a pleasure," replied the older bear, with a smile.

CHAPTER XVI

MR. P. H. ANTELOPE AT ROOSEVELT LODGE

BACK at Tower Falls, Cubby and his mother told everyone they met about their wonderful experience. They saw the Civilized Bear again, sitting in his window being admired, and then wandering out to have his picture taken.

"We'll be getting on," said Mommie Bear. "If we do not hurry, old Jack Frost will be around!" They sat for awhile under a great cliff that overhung the road. They knew it was called the "Over Hanging Cliff" for they heard the people talk of it as they passed. Nor did the people forget to notice Cubby. They would even turn from the beautiful things about them to look at the little bear.

Cubby and Mommie Bear saw the Needle, a tall slender spire of rock, with its eye at the river's edge and its point three hundred feet up in the air. There were many oddly formed rocks. Some that looked like towers from castle walls.

"I have looked up so much," said Cubby, "that my neck hurts. How strange that great rocks should be here, holding their heads so high! I'm glad that the old giant that gathered up the stones did not come this way."

"Perhaps he did," said Mommie Bear. "It is the river that has made these wonderful formations. After all, the water is a giant too and had giant strength. It must be very firm, solid rock to stand like that without crumbling."

When they moved on, they found that the cars were turning off to a lodge k n o w n as the Roosevelt Lodge. Mommie Bear learned that this was a splendid place for fishing. The scenery was beautiful and there was much wild life. "We will stay here," said she.

There was something very restful about the place and in the days that followed neither Cubby nor his mother spoke of moving on. They found deep thickets in which to sleep undisturbed through long, quiet hours. They found many of their relations, and in their long trips about the country had peeps at many of the

Some looked like towers

wild things that called this place home. Here they met the dainty little prong-horned antelope and learned just how his family was different from any other antelope in all the world.

Mr. P. H. Antelope told them about it himself. He was very proud of his initials. He said they stood for Prong Horn. Cubby thought it a rather odd name, but being polite he didn't say anything about it. When he heard that the members of this family were the only ones in the world to have a prong or branch on their horns, he was very much interested.

"I would be proud too, Mr. P. H. Antelope," said Cubby, "if I had anything like that about me. I don't wonder at all that you like us to remember your initials."

"Our family all live in America," the pretty creature told him. "There are antelopes that live in other countries but they are not P. H. Antelopes," and Mr. P. H. Antelope blinked his great eyes knowingly.

"And do you take off your horns like Mr. Moose?" asked Cubby, earnestly.

"Yes and no," answered Mr. P. H. Antelope. "We do and we don't. Our horns are hollow and we shed the outer sheath. Mr. Moose's horns are solid and he sheds them all. He sheds his in the early spring or winter and we shed ours in the fall. We"—and he hesitated a moment—"well, I hate to brag, but," and he held his head very high, "we are the only hollow-horned animals in the world that shed their horns!"

"Is that so?" said Cubby in just the right tone. For

Cubby was interested in learning about his wild neighbors, and he was very, very much impressed.

"Have you seen our deer?" asked Mr. P. H. Antelope.

"Not yet," said Cubby, "but Mommie Bear thinks we may any day."

"I hope you will," said his new friend. "They are very pretty but shy. I am shy, too. I do not usually have anything to do with bears. This is very unlike me."

Cubby chuckled. "I guess Mommie and I are different too,"

Mr. P. H. Antelope

he said. "Most bears care only for eating and do not waste much time visiting with their neighbors or looking at the scenery."

And Cubby did see the deer, a mother deer with her little spotted fawn. They stood for a moment and looked at Cubby with gentle, frightened eyes and then were lost in the deep green of the forest.

Before Cubby and Mommie Bear left the region about Roosevelt Lodge they had seen many, many of the wild creatures that lived so happily hidden away in the dense wilderness that spread all about.

"I am glad that we stopped here," said Mommie Bear, "for now you have met and know so many of the children of the Park. It is important for you to know who are your friends and who are your enemies. Now we will go on."

"I have loved it here," said Cubby. "Even the people who stopped here seemed interested in all kinds of animals. And all the wild things seem more friendly. I'd like to live here myself."

"Perhaps you will wish to come back here and make this your home," said Mommie Bear. "We will see all we can and then you shall decide where you will be the happiest."

CHAPTER XVII

THE PETRIFIED TREE

MOMMIE BEAR with Cubby at her heels was shambling along up the trail.

"You are going to see a petrified tree this morning," said Mommie.

"A petrified tree!" repeated Cubby. "What do you suppose it is? Have I ever seen one?"

"I do not believe you have, sonny," his mother said, "and neither have I. We will know more about it when we see and taste of it."

"Do we taste of trees?" asked Cubby.

"Of course," said Mommie Bear. "I knew there was something I had neglected teaching you. You know the nice thick coat that the trees wear is called bark. But underneath the bark is something very good and sweet. I will show you how to bite and tear away the bark and eat the sweet under the bark. I think we will take the petrified tree for your first lesson so you will always remember it. Here is a sign. I think it is the one that tells us to turn off from the main road to see the tree. I am glad that we have come early for we shall not be bothered by people while I am giving you your lesson."

"I am glad too, Mommie Bear," said Cubby, "for you are so timid that you would never show me if there were any people watching us."

93

At last they reached the spot. "Well," said Mommie Bear, "it looks very strange, does it not? It has lost its branches but it is still standing, or at least its trunk is still standing. There is something very queer about this tree, Cubby."

"Very queer?" repeated Cubby. "Of course, Mommie, it is petrified, whatever that may be. A sort of a pet tree, I imagine, like a pet bear or a pet woodchuck. There were ever so many pet woodchucks back at the Lodge."

But his Mommie shook her head. "This tree is dead. A tree cannot live without leaves and branches. But perhaps I can show you, just the same, about tearing the bark, and we will find a living tree later for you to taste the sweet underbark. Now watch closely, Cubby. I take hold of the bark down at the foot of the tree. I bite in quickly with all my strength so as to get a firm hold and then I pull back and tear the bark away from the tree. Now, I will show you." She bent her head to the base of the tree and made a quick sudden movement! And then she dropped back and raised her paws to her mouth.

"What is the matter?" called Cubby in alarm.

Mommie Bear shook her head. "Oh," she said, "my teeth, I hurt them. That bark is so hard. I never saw anything like it in all my life." She turned again to the tree and sniffed.

In a moment she turned to Cubby with big round eyes.

"Cubby," she said, softly, "it isn't a tree at all. It's a stone."

Cubby looked. "But see, Mommie Bear," he cried, "there is the bark, just like a real tree."

"Put your nose against it," said Mommie Bear. So Cubby put his little nose against it—and it was cold! He turned to his mother. Bark would have been different. This was stone!

"It's a stone tree," he whispered. "Now, what giant made it? An ice giant or a water giant? It never was a tree."

"We will wait," said Mommie Bear. "Soon there will be people coming. If we listen to what they say, we may learn how it came to be here."

So Cubby and his mother waited. While they looked about they found other smaller stone trees. But soon a car drove into the clearing. "Good," said Mommie Bear. "There are children—they will ask questions." So Cubby and his mother sat near and listened.

"It can't be stone," said a little girl, "it looks like a real tree."

"That's because it's petrified," said her older brother, glad to tell what he knew. "Petrified trees look like real trees."

"But it couldn't have ever been alive," cried the little girl. "It's just one of those funny stones that look like something else."

"It was alive," said the boy; "wasn't it, mother?"

"Once a lovely green tree stood here," said mother,

"long, long years ago. We do not know how long. And then something happened. A soft mud came flowing through the forest. It came from a volcano. Stones were hurled through the air. Clouds of dust settled over the trees until they were covered. The branches and leaves fell and there they lay buried in the mud. In this mud was something called silica. As the wood of the tree dissolved it soaked up the water from the mud. A little bit of the silica took the place of each tiny particle of wood. No air could reach the tree so it rotted slowly, and there was so much pressure that the silica was pushed into every tiny crevice. And now, thousands of years later, when the mud has dried and crumbled away we find this petrified stump still standing, but it is stone although it is shaped just like the old tree. One can see every detail."

"How wonderful!" said the little girl.

"There are some wonderful fossil forests to be seen in the Park," said the children's father, "but they are hard to reach. I have read that the petrified trees here in the Park are the only ones ever found standing as they grew. One can find petrified wood almost anywhere but not trunks of trees standing like this one. I am glad that you children have had a chance to see it."

"But what made the mud flow?" asked the little girl.

"It came from a volcano," said her mother. "Long ago there were many of them here. The heat inside the earth made steam from the water. The steam is strong; it pushed up."

"Like a big bubble of hot mush," explained the brother.

"Yes, something like that. You know steam is strong and it pushes and finds a way out. So the mud and hot water came boiling out of the top of a mountain, and the mud ran down the slopes. I suppose it cooled somewhat before it reached these trees or the wood would have been burned."

"Oh, I see," said the little girl. "And now these petrified trees stand here to tell the story of that long-ago time."

"That's it exactly," said her mother. "They tell us the story of a day long ago when trees stood green and beautiful in the sun, until this wonderful thing happened."

"I don't think it was wonderful," said the boy; "I think it was dreadful."

"It is one of the ways the world has been made," said the mother. "It is God's plan. The tree would have been gone thousands of years ago if this had not happened, but here it is to-day in a petrified form for us to look at and to wonder over."

"Look," said the boy, "there is a bear and its cub. Why, I would almost believe they were listening to us. They sit with such an intelligent look on their faces. Perhaps they were as curious as you were, sis."

"They do look interested," said the father. "The way to learn is to ask. I do not want you to go through this wonderland with your eyes shut. Look about you and ask about the things you do not understand. Perhaps your mother and I may not be able to tell you all you want to know, but we can ask, too, and find out. You've learned something about petrified trees anyway."

"I'd like to ask," said the boy, "about the kinds of trees they find petrified. Can they tell that from the fossils?"

"Yes," said his father. "They find many different kinds, some that do not grow here at all now. Walnut and hickory trees, redwoods, figs, and breadfruit. Oh, many others too. They all help tell the story of that long-ago day."

"Those trees grow in a warmer climate than this," said the boy in surprise.

"That's just it," said the father. "The remains of those old trees tell us that in that day so long ago it was warmer here than it is now or they would not have been here. It is a wonderful story the fossils and the rocks have to tell us. Perhaps as you grow older you will want to learn more about it."

"I will," said the boy. "After all, right here about us is the story of the world, for us to study, and it is not written in a book."

"We are reading now out of Mother Nature's lovely storybook," said his mother. "Aren't we glad that we came to the Park? But we must go on, for we have not all summer to look. The wonderful Mammoth Hot Springs come next, you know."

Cubby and his mother watched them go to their car.

But they did not leave until they had rummaged among their things and tossed out a handful of cookies to the two bears.

"Well, I have learned something," said Mommie Bear, going to the tree and sniffing. "A petrified tree! I'm the one that will never forget this lesson. And to think I expected to eat it! I am very humiliated. No bear in the world would do such a thing."

"I'm glad we couldn't eat it," said Cubby. "After standing here for all those thousands of years it would be a shame to eat it up."

"And spoil one of the pages in Mother Nature's storybook," grinned Mommie Bear. "I'm glad too, Cubby. But come now and I'll give you your lesson on a tree that isn't petrified."

CHAPTER XVIII

A CURIOUS CUBBY

MOMMIE BEAR taught Cubby how to strip the bark from the tree and eat the under bark. "This tastes the best in spring and early summer," she told him. "The sap is coming from the roots of the trees then and there is much rich juice."

"I will remember," said Cubby as they traveled along. It was wonderful, the trip to Mammoth Hot Springs. Cubby and his mother often sat down and just looked at the scenery about them. At last they reached Gardiner River and crossed over the long steel bridge. Cubby had learned to love bridges and was delighted to find such a splendid big one, the largest one in the Park.

And then it was not far to Mammoth Hot Springs. As they wandered into the little settlement of houses at the foot of the mountains they were pleased to see that others of their family were already there. They admired the lovely hotel with its broad porches.

"We have come a long way," said Mommie Bear. "We will rest and get acquainted before we start out to see the sights." So they wandered down past the Museum building, where people were coming and going.

"I wonder what they see there," said Cubby. "It

must be something of interest. After all, people can see some things that bears can't."

"Look here, sonny," said his mother, "do see this little building made of horns. Isn't it cunning?"

"Why, it is," said Cubby, "just built of horns. There are some of Mr. Moose's antlers. We'll tell him when we see him again."

"Yes, and there are elk horns and some pretty little deer horns. And there are some antelope horns too."

"Some of Mr. P. H. Antelope's," giggled Cubby. "Do you remember him, Mommie, and how proud he was of his name, P. H. for 'prong-horned'—the only antelope with a prong on his horns?"

"I certainly do," answered Mommie Bear, "and the only hollow-horned animal to shed his horns. After all, Cubby, I guess we have seen a lot of things the people haven't seen, although we cannot go into hotels and museums. Let us rest here in this sunny house awhile. But look, here comes that family we met at the petrified tree. I believe they are going to take our picture."

Mommie Bear was so interested that she stood right up on her hind legs and Cubby stood right beside her with one little paw resting on her hip. There they stood and waited. But nothing happened only the mother who held the little black box with the shiny eye looked up and laughed and said that it ought to be "splendid."

Cubby wondered what ought to be splendid, but he did not find out; so after waiting a minute he and his mother moved along down the trail toward the house-keeping cabins. They had learned from the other bears not to call them "dens."

Cubby was very much puzzled over the little pipes fastened to the sides of the cabins—not on every cabin, but here and there among them. He wondered what they were for. In a little while a lady came, carrying a pail. She turned something on the pipe, and at once a clear stream of water ran into the pail. Cubby was amazed. He had never seen anything like it before, although his mother told him that at all the other camps there had been the same plan for getting water.

"Well," said Cubby, "these people do not like trouble. That's one thing sure. Just think, they do not need to go down to the river when they want a drink. There is no telling what else they may have for their comfort. Some day I am going into one of those cabins and look around."

"Just remember Meddlesome," said his mother. "I know Meddlesome would be in one of those cabins in a minute if he had a chance. He is a curious little cub. Most cubs are, for that matter, but I must say, Cubby, that you are a very good little bear. You have not given me trouble or made me worried or anxious. Often I have seen cubs who were always in trouble and sometimes they would get their mothers into trouble too because they were so naughty."

"But I would like to look in," Cubby said, wistfully. "I wouldn't touch a thing."

Mommie Bear shook her head. "It's wiser to stay out. Now I am going to lie here in the sun and take a little nap. You be a good little bear and amuse yourself without getting into mischief." So she lay down and soon was sleeping deeply.

Cubby looked about. The little log cabins stood in neat rows or streets, and each door had a number. "I suppose," thought Cubby, "that is how they tell them apart, for they do look just exactly alike, and it would be so easy to forget just which cabin you lived in. And then a car drove up to the door of the cabin across the street. Cubby watched the people get out and carry their things into the cabin. They seemed so happy.

"This is a lovely cabin," said a little girl. "Grandma, do come and see how nice and clean it is inside. And, oh, there is a stove and two lovely beds!"

"To be sure," said a pleasant lady who seemed to be the "Grandma." "It is so much fun sleeping in a cabin made of logs. Doesn't it have a nice, clean, piney smell in here? Let's open the windows."

Cubby sat and watched. It was almost as much fun as going in. He could see them carrying in their blankets from the car and making up the beds. This puzzled him, but he remembered that as people did not wear fur coats they would need something warm on their beds. He watched them cook their meal over the funny low stove. For the little girl's father had brought wood from the wood cafeteria, a place where wood cut in just the right lengths were sold to the people. The food smelled very good and the family looked very happy as they sat about eating.

And then they washed the dishes and packed the food away. The father went away to look about the place and the Grandma sat outside in the car reading. The little girl played about the door.

"They are very happy," thought Cubby. "I will just move a little nearer and see if they would not like a little bear to play with."

So he edged a little closer. No one seemed to notice, and Mommie Bear lay very quiet, her deep breathing telling him that she still slept. So Cubby went nearer. Now he was almost at the door. In a minute he would be inside—he would really be in a cabin!

But something happened. The Grandmother stepped quickly from the car and into the doorway. The little girl cried out in a shrill voice, and—bang!—the door slammed in his face! It was a terrible bang! Cubby had never known that doors could speak so loudly. He shrank back—and there stood his mother! How strange she looked! Her fur seemed to have puffed up and she was standing with an angry light in her eyes and a deep grumble in her throat. He could hardly believe that she was his own Mommie Bear. He ran quickly to her. And then Cubby told her the truth. He told her just what he had done. He told her about the loud noise of the slammed door.

For a little while his mother did not answer and then she said, slowly: "I know, Cubby, that your feelings are hurt. You thought they would like you to come in."

"Yes," sobbed Cubby, "people always seemed to like me."

"But they do not want you in their cabins any more than we would want them to come into our dens. After this you will understand. Now you know what I mean when I talk about cubs that make their mothers trouble. You frightened me and I woke with a start. I didn't know for a moment where you were. I thought something had happened to you. I was angry and I might have done something that I would have been sorry for if you had not come quickly to me. I hope you will never do this again."

"I hope I never will either," said Cubby. "But see, Mommie, I guess the people are not angry. They have thrown out some food for us. Perhaps they are sorry that they frightened us and I am sorry that I frightened them."

"Then we will forget it," said Mommie Bear. "I have had my nap and we will go along now and see what there is to be seen."

CHAPTER XIX

FAIRY COLORS AT MAMMOTH HOT SPRINGS

THERE was a great deal to be seen, and Cubby and his mother followed a group of people as they wound their way up a mountainside. The path was often narrow, and every now and then they stopped to look about them. Everybody stopped to look at a great cone-shaped formation forty feet high. "That's the Liberty Cap," someone said.

Then as they moved along they came to a series of steps covered with something white. These steps were called a "terrace."

"What makes them so white?" asked Cubby, cuddling close to his mother's side.

"Once water went over these steps," Mommie Bear told him. "It carried lime and this

"That's the Liberty Cap," someone said

lime has settled over everything. It looks as if the water were still running."

"It looks to me as if the water had frozen while it was running," said Cubby. "It seems like a great mass of ice with the icicles dripping over the edges of the steps."

"It does," said Mommie Bear; and so they went on and on together watching very carefully where they stepped. They saw many hot springs and caves where hot water gushed forth.

"It reminds me a little of the Naughty Elf back at the Dragon's Mouth cave," said Cubby. "Do you suppose he is still growling and grumbling?"

"I suppose so," said Mommie Bear. "But there are many more of them here and much more wonderful."

At last they reached the Angel Terrace, thought to be one of the most beautiful anywhere. Cubby wondered what made the colorings in the water so beautiful. "I have never seen such lovely water before," he told his mother, happily. They stood at last near the blue springs and could look down over the pools and terraces.

"See," he cried waving a little furry paw, "there is green, and yonder is yellow, and there is a beautiful blue, and even a peach color. Did you ever, Mommie Bear, see anything like it?"

"I never have," said his mother. "We must try to find out why it is so. If we hurry, perhaps we can overtake that group of people and hear just why it is."

"Then let us hurry," said Cubby.

So they hurried and reached the group of people just

in time to hear the guide say: "Now, if you will look down over the pools, springs and terraces as they lie before us, you can see the different colorings very well. It is almost like a bit of fairyland, and it is really hard to believe that the colors are made by tiny plants growing in the water."

"It looks as if the water were still running"

"Plants," whispered Cubby, to his mother, "why, whoever would have thought it!"

"Hush," said Mommie Bear, "we must hear how that can be."

"The plants," said the guide, "are called algae; they are very tiny, and grow in hot water. When the water is quite hot, the plants are white; a little cooler and they turn yellow. When the water is still a little cooler, they are orange color, and as it cools more and more we find such pretty colors as pink and red and then green. People who have studied the pools can tell how hot the water is by its color. Look at that pool yonder and see the colors change as the water cools at the outside edges. It looks like a rainbow!"

Cubby thought that it did too, for he had often seen splendid rainbows.

The man went on to tell that some of the pools were too hot for the little plants, so it was not found in them. He said that sometimes the pools with the yellow plants and the blue sky overhead made the water green, just as though one had mixed the colors. Cubby and Mommie Bear did not move on with the people. They wanted to stay and watch the rainbow lights.

"I wonder," thought Cubby, "if one should dip up a little of the water would it be green like the water in the pool?" He kept looking and he kept thinking about it. At last he thrust his furry little paw down toward the pool.

But before it reached the water Mommie Bear had given him a quick push away. "What are you trying to do, Cubby, burn yourself so we cannot go on and see the rest of the Park? Dear me, that water is very hot— almost boiling. That is a deep pool, one of the yellow-plant kind that blends with the sky."

"I only wanted to see if the water would be colored," whimpered Cubby. "I thought if I put my paw in it, I would have a green paw. It would be fun to have a pretty colored coat like the butterflies."

"You silly little bear," laughed his mother. "You would have had a burned paw, not a green one. If you dipped up that water it would be just like any other water. Didn't you hear the man say that it is the little plants and the blue sky that make it seem green? How glad I am that I saw you just in time! You must be very careful around these hot pools and springs."

Cubby and Mommie Bear spent many days at the springs. They liked to follow the trail around the springs and never grew tired of looking at the colors in the pools. They loved the old Jupiter Terrace too, and were so glad they had seen it, for one day they heard the guide say that it was the largest hot spring terrace in the world.

They met other bears at the bear pits, where garbage was brought from the hotels. But most of them were only interested in what they could find to eat. However, one day they met a stranger.

"I've just come, and I feel very new and strange," he told Cubby and his mother. "You see, I came in by the northern entrance."

"We came by the southern," said Mommie Bear. "We have come a long way. Is it far to the northern entrance?"

"About five miles," said the newcomer. "Through a very pretty country too. I came through Gardiner Canyon. It is very rugged with high gray walls. I saw the Eagle Nest Rock. Have you seen it?"

"No," said Mommie Bear. "Tell us about it."

"It is a great high rocky cliff with one column stretching up all alone, high above the rest. It makes a safe place for birds to nest. I heard that though it is called Eagle Nest Rock osprey nests are seen there more often than eagles."

"We saw some of them back at the Yellowstone Canyon," said Cubby, eagerly. "Don't you remember, Mommie Bear? They catch fish. They have their nests in tall trees or high cliffs."

"You are right," said the newcomer, and Mommie Bear nodded her head. "Those are the birds that nest in the great top of Eagle Nest Cliff. Everyone stops to look up and see them."

"Can't we go there?" said Cubby.

"Another summer perhaps we may," said Mommie Bear, "but we must go on now. I am anxious to get to Old Faithful, whatever that is. I hear it spoken of so often and want to see it for myself." Then she explained to the other bear, "We did not go to see the buffalo here, as we had such a fine view of them in their wild state on a trip we took from Tower Falls."

"I think I will take a look at these," said the new bear. "I may not have a chance to see them again. Have you enjoyed your trip here?"

"Oh, very much," said Cubby, eagerly, before Mommie Bear could say a word, and he told about the pretty colors that were made from the little plants that liked to live in hot water.

Cubby could have talked and talked, but Mommie

Bear thought they should go to bed early because on the next day they would travel far. So they told their new friend good-by and pushed out into the wilderness to find a nice snug place in which to sleep.

CHAPTER XX

THE TWO GIANTS OF THE HOODOOS

MOMMIE BEAR and Cubby hated to tell Mammoth Hot Springs good-by. "I'll never forget the rainbow water," said Cubby, wistfully as they turned back to take their last view of the wonderland they had so enjoyed. "But I will not look back any more—I will look forward. I know we shall find something that will make us very happy."

They did not have long to wait. They had shambled along but a few miles when they came to such a strange land.

"It looks," said Cubby, "as if someone had picked up the world and shaken it. Do look, Mommie! Did you ever see such a tumbled heap of big bowlders? Do you suppose," he hurried on, "that this is another trick of that ice giant?"

Mommie Bear had stopped in her tracks. "No, sonny," she said, "these bowlders do not look rounded like the ones the ice giant carried. If they had been carried, their edges would have been worn away. These are rough and broken. What a strange topsy-turvy land this is! And do you know what I am thinking?"

"What are you thinking, Mommie?" said Cubby, eagerly.

"I'm thinking what splendid dens there must be under some of these great boulders. I can easily imagine there must be some wonderful caves here. I suppose this is what they call 'The Hoodoos'—and this is the Silver Gate where the road is cut through."

The Silver Gate

"It seems very strange," said Cubby, "that all these great rocks could be thrown down in this way. It must have been the work of something very, very strong. You think it is not the ice giant; do you suppose it was a water giant, or a steam giant like those the lady told about back at the petrified tree?"

"I do not know," said Mommie Bear, "but if you want to make a story about it, Cubby, go ahead and do it."

"I'll think about it," said Cubby. "Perhaps I can think of something later."

"I have seen rocks," said Mommie Bear, "but never such big ones or so many all tumbled about like this. My, my! We keep moving along and here they still are —ever and ever so many! It must have been a great deal of trouble to make this road. You can see for yourself, Cubby, that lots of great rocks have had to be broken up and moved out of the way. But, then, people seem to be able to do almost anything. We do get along faster walking down the road than if we clambered over the rocks."

"I'm afraid I couldn't clamber over some of them," said Cubby, "they look, oh, so big to me."

"I guess you couldn't," said Mommie Bear. "But we are seeing things, aren't we, Cubby dear! And, now, what is this?" she asked.

"Oh," cried Cubby, "how lovely! This must be the Golden Gateway. How beautiful that great wall is! It is colored like the rainbow water back at the falls only there is more gold than anything else. Rocks can be so different and so pretty. I love them all."

"Let us cross over to the other side of the canyon," said Mommie Bear, "and look back at this. I am tired. We will spend the night there. Perhaps we may find some ripe berries."

So Cubby and his mother left the road and crossed over to the wild side of the mountain. There was a cool stream at the bottom of the canyon and a wooded slope beyond, and, yes, there were berries—lovely sweet, red, ripe raspberries! Cubby did not have to be told what to do. He just gave one sniff and sat down in the middle of the patch. He opened his arms and gathered into them all the bushes that he possibly could and then hold-

ing them tightly he stood up. As he rose he stripped every leaf and every berry from the stalk! He held his arms tight and bent his head to gobble up all the delicious food in his arms. He didn't mind the leaves, for oh, the berries were so sweet. And when he had eaten every bit he sat down again and did it all over!

Lovely sweet, red, ripe raspberries!

He forgot all about Mommie Bear for a while, but when he turned his head, there she was in a raspberry thicket doing exactly the same thing. She did look so funny and he had to stop and laugh.

Then she turned her head and saw Cubby. And she laughed. "Cubby," she called, "what is that you have on your fur coat?" Cubby looked down and saw that he was quite covered with the juice of the berries, so he began licking the sweet drops with his tongue. It was quite too good to waste a single bit.

"I think, Mommie Bear," he said, "that this is a lovely place to stay for a few days."

"I think so too," said Mommie Bear; "we will stay anyway as long as we can find plenty of berries."

And so they picked their berries bear fashion until it was time to go to bed and then slept happily under the stars.

CHAPTER XXI

THE GIANTS' STORY

CUBBY and his mother were content to spend many days of the long summer resting and hunting for food. "Perhaps we shall enjoy the scenery even more after this rest," Mommie Bear told her little son. "We have seen so much. I like to lie in the sun and think over the many wonderful things we have seen together. Have you thought of a story yet for the hoodoos—the great rocks that lie scattered over the mountainside that we passed?"

But Cubby shook his head.

"I have thought of one," said Mommie Bear. "It was a giant. It must have been a very great giant—perhaps several giants, who knows? I have started the story but I cannot finish it. Shall I tell you how it starts?"

"Yes, do," said Cubby, sleepily. "I like stories about giants. Perhaps I can help you finish it."

"Once upon a time," began Mommie Bear, "there were two giants. They were very strong—oh, very, very strong. It was all a long, long time ago. Maybe as long ago as when the tree that is now petrified was so beautiful and green. I do not know how long ago it was, but it doesn't matter.

"Now, each giant had a mountain. And each giant thought his mountain was finer than the other. And they liked to slide down their mountains. You remember how that little Mrs. Otter loved to slide. I think these giants loved it as much as she.

"So every day they came out to slide down their mountains. They would often race. And after awhile one would become angry when the other beat him. And sometimes they quarreled. Then the mountains would ring with their angry voices. It was like the thundering of a great storm. And all their friends would warn them and say: 'Oh, you two great giants must not quarrel. You are too big. If you should fight, something might happen that would make you very sorry.' But the giants would not listen.

" 'He's not going to beat me,' said one. 'I think he started sooner than he should. He has to be fair.' And the other giant said the very same thing. Everyone was worried. Even Mother Nature came and talked to them.

" 'Listen,' she said, 'if you do not stop quarreling, you may hurt my pretty world.' But they would not listen and only quarreled harder than ever.

"At last they both grew so angry that they came to blows. It was very sad to see such great giants fighting. The whole world trembled, and then a dreadful thing happened. The mountains tumbled down, just like a great heap of blocks! The huge stones rolled here and there all over the place."

"And the giants," interrupted Cubby, "were they hurt?"

"Hardly at all," said Mommie Bear. "One of them had a little bump on his head and the other one, well a boulder rolled on his big toe. But they really were not hurt much. That is, nothing except their feelings. They felt so sorry that their two lovely mountains were gone that they sat down and cried for days and days and days. Their tears made all the rivers rise. And when they stopped crying and looked up there was Mother Nature looking at them.

" 'You have spoiled two of my loveliest mountains,' she said, so sadly that the two giants almost began to cry again, only she begged them not to. I suppose they felt as sorry as we would have felt if we had eaten the petrified tree. That is, if we could have eaten it. You remember how surprised I was when I tried?"

"I certainly do," said Cubby, laughing.

"Well, the two giants were very, very sorry.

" 'We will pick them up,' said the first giant. 'We will put them all in a nice pile and make new mountains out of them,' he promised. But Mother Nature shook her head.

" 'No,' she said, 'they probably wouldn't stick together and would come rolling down and hurt some of my wild children. It's best to leave them as they are. Whenever you see them, though, remember that when one loses his temper, he is apt to do something for which he will always be sorry.'

"The two great giants hung their heads. 'What can we do?' they asked. 'We want to do something to show how sorry we are.'

" 'This is to be my Park,' said Mother Nature, 'I have been planning to make it a wonderland for all my children. Suppose you find something very wonderful and bring it here to make people happy. Then we will have something to take the place of my two pretty mountains.'

" 'We will try,' said the two giants, and so they set out in the world to find something that would make the Park even more beautiful than it had been before the two mountains tumbled down. That is as far as I can go," said Mommie Bear. "I don't know what they found. But perhaps we will find out as we go along."

"I'm really quite excited over it," said Cubby. "Perhaps we should be getting on. We have had some lovely days here. The berries have been delicious. And didn't you like the little bit of honey we found?"

"It was delicious, too," said Mommie Bear. "It is too bad there are not more bees in the Park."

"If those two giants had wanted to bring something to make the bears happy," said Cubby, "they might have brought in a lot of bees to make all the honey we could eat."

"I don't believe they ever tasted honey," said Mommie Bear.

Each day they moved on farther toward the south. Now the nights were cooler but the days were warm and sunny. The birds had nested and the little ones were hunting food for themselves.

"We'll go on," said Mommie Bear, "we'll have to keep moving now. For winter is around the corner—and we must find what the two giants brought."

CHAPTER XXII

A MOUNTAIN OF GLASS

MOMMIE BEAR and Cubby had gone several miles past the Golden Gates when suddenly they came to the mountain of glass. It was more like a great cliff, perhaps, but it rose high above their heads. The people called it the Obsidian Cliff, but Cubby didn't call it anything. It was just like a mountain of jet-black polished glass.

Mommie Bear could hardly believe her eyes. "I have never seen anything like this," she told Cubby. "I've seen stones and stones and rocks and rocks and bowlders and bowlders, but nothing like this. Do you suppose this is what the two giants brought?"

"No, I don't think so," said Cubby, "although it is very wonderful and strange. There is a lovely lake here, Mommie. See how pretty this glass mountain looks in its clear waters."

"We will see if there are any fish here," said Mommie Bear. She turned to look at the lake. "Oh, Cubby," she cried, "here are beavers! Now you shall see something interesting."

And there was much to see and hear. Cubby and his mother met little Bessie Beaver, who told them about her life in the river.

123

"No," said Bessie Beaver, "I have never been through the Park. I have been much too busy. We beavers are workers. We are builders too. What do bears build?"

"Why," said Mommie Bear, "I'm sure I don't know. I don't remember of ever having built anything."

Bessie Beaver looked very surprised. "Do you live in the river?" she asked.

"No," said Mommie Bear. "We can swim but we do not live in the water.

"We do," said Bessie Beaver, proudly. "Of course we live out of the water too, but we depend on the water. We have a lovely home yonder. Do you see its roof sticking out of the water?"

"Oh, yes," said Cubby, "but where is the door?"

"Why, under the water of course," laughed Bessie Beaver. "We swim into our houses. One of the reasons that we are so safe is because our doorway is under water. That is why we build a dam. If it should break, the water would run away and our doorway would be open. And if the water is not deep our doorway might freeze over in winter so we could not get out for food."

"You are very clever," said Mommie Bear, "to build such a nice home. Cubby and I cannot go in and see it, but will you tell us about it, Bessie Beaver?"

"We have more than one door," said Bessie. "It is safer, you know, to have more than one door. Our rooms have sloping floors so the water can run back into the pond. Of course we swim into the house and bring some water in on our fur. Our beds are in the highest part of the rooms. We make them up with fine grasses and wood and bark. Oh, we shred every bit very fine and soft. Our houses are plastered with mud inside so they are very warm."

"How do you get air?" asked Mommie Bear. "With the water up over your doorway and the walls of your house so tight I should think you would smother."

Bessie Beaver

Bessie Beaver laughed. "We have thought of that too, Mrs. Bear. We cut a little hole in our roof to let the bad air out and the good air in. In winter you can see the steam rising from this little hole. Old sly fox often comes and says, 'Bessie Beaver, Bessie Beaver, may I come in?' And I say, 'No, no, no, not by the hair of my chin, chin, chin.' Then says sly fox, 'I'll huff and I'll puff and I'll blow your house in.' Well, then we all just laugh and laugh. We say: 'Draw a deep breath, old sly fox, for you will need it. You never can blow this house in, for it is made so strong from logs and branches and is so well plastered with mud. Now that it is frozen you can never blow it in or dig it in or get in at all. Be off with you.' But, dear me, there comes Bobby Beaver now, he is carrying mud to plaster up a new room in our house. See, he carries it under his chin! I must run and help him."

"Wait a minute," said Mommie Bear; "can you tell us something about this glass mountain? Cubby and I want to know where it came from."

Bessie Beaver looked over at the shining glass walls of Obsidian Cliff. "It has been there ever since any of our people can remember," she said. "I think it is lovely. Some strange people used to come long ago for bits of it. They were red people. I think they called them Indians. Of course I do not remember them, for that was long before I came to live here. But I have heard the old beavers talk of it, for their parents told them, and their parents told them. You see, it is a story of many years ago. They say the Indians came to get the glass to make their arrow heads."

"Well, well," said Mommie Bear. "I have seen Indians myself. It was not so long ago that we saw no other people but the Indians. It is true that they used to use bows and arrows. No doubt this glass would make very fine arrow heads."

"I think it would," said Bessie Beaver. "Anyway it's very pretty. All the tourists who pass look at our black glass mountain and sometimes they forget to look at us.

That just suits us, for we do not like to be bothered. But now I really must be going, Bobby Beaver will be wondering what has kept me. Good-by and I hope you have a nice time in the Park."

"Beavers are smart," said Cubby as they watched Bessie disappear in the water. "Who would think that a little animal like that could plan and make such a home? I would like to know more about them. Perhaps we can come this way again when Bessie is not so busy."

A little farther on they came to another mountain. It was not a glass mountain but a smoking mountain. Mommie Bear was alarmed at first. Smoke seemed to be rising over it. She sat down and looked for a long time at the strange sight. She sniffed the air. At last she said: "It isn't smoke, Cubby, it is steam. Those trees have died from heat but they are not burned. Oh, son, this is a strange land indeed. We will keep to the roadway. It is the safest."

Just then a car stopped near them. This is Roaring Mountain, they heard someone say. "Once it was covered with lovely trees, but the steam began to come through the ground and made it like this. The guidebook says this happened only about thirty years ago. Think of that!"

Cubby smiled at his mother and she smiled back. "Then this was not what the great giants brought," said Mommie Bear, "for they lived long ago."

"That's just what I was thinking," said Cubby. "As soon as I saw this Roaring Mountain I wondered if it could be the wonderful thing they brought to the Park. But it was something else, I feel sure. I am glad, aren't you, Mommie Bear? It will be fun to keep on looking."

"Yes," said Mommie Bear, "it will, although I do think these two mountains, the glass mountain and this burning one, are wonderful."

As they moved on they saw many strange things. There were two lakes lying close together, with a little brook connecting them, but one lake was blue and the other was green. "We know," said Cubby happily, "that it is the tiny plants that make the color."

"Let us not wait," said Mommie Bear. "I wish to get on to the next hotel. But it surely is interesting here. Everywhere we look we see steaming things. All the springs are boiling."

"There must be heaps of fairy people with their bubbling mud roofs here," said Cubby. "I wonder, Mommie Bear, if there are not some nice steam-heated dens here too?"

"I wouldn't be surprised," said Mommie Bear. "Now that we have seen so much steam we know what it is. It is strange that good old-fashioned water can turn into steam."

"And become a giant," said Cubby, "for steam is strong, we have learned. How wonderful it is that water can take fairy shapes and go floating off as though it had wings! Why, it's as wonderful as the little worm that turns into a lovely butterfly. Do you suppose I'll ever turn into anything, Mommie Bear?"

"Just into a big bear, instead of a little one," laughed his mother, "though that's a wonderful thing too. But it is late, sonny. See, the shadows have fallen. I do not

Roaring Mountain

think I want to sleep here until I have had more time to look about. We will go on until we come to the next camp."

"But it's getting dark, Mommie Bear, and I'm afraid we will miss a lot of lovely things," said Cubby. "Suppose we should go right by the wonderful thing that the two giants brought?"

"We can come back by daylight," said his mother, comforting him. "But I am hungry now; there will be food at the camp." So they went on together through the darkness.

CHAPTER XXIII

OLD FAITHFUL

MOMMIE BEAR and Cubby saw the lights from the great hotel long before they reached it. When they got there Mommie said, "Why this is the Old Faithful Inn, said to be the largest log structure in all the world. Someone, I think it was Mrs. Otter, told me that seven hundred people can be comfortably cared for here."

"My!" said Cubby. "Think of seven hundred bears in one den!"

"I would rather think of something else," said Cubby's mother. "Just see the cars parked by the side of the road!"

"Yes, and yonder is a great crowd of people," said Cubby, eagerly. "I wonder what they are looking at?"

"We will find out," said Mommie Bear. So they hurried to join the group of people. "It is a bubbling spring," said she as they drew nearer. "See the steam rising!"

They had come just in time, for now the boiling grew fiercer! The hot water leaped higher and higher! Cubby could not believe his eyes. What was going to happen? Suddenly there was a roar, and up shot a mighty column of water and steam—up, up, up! Oh, it

was beautiful! And yet it was so great and so unex-
pected that Cubby, standing on his little hind legs beside his mother, lost his balance and fell completely over.

A light from the hotel played upon the great column
of water and steam that seemed to rise to the very
heavens and made rainbow colors in the steam clouds.
And then—it was gone.
Only a little puff of
steam marked the spot
where the great column
had risen.

For a long time Mom-
mie Bear and Cubby
stood watching, think-
ing that perhaps it
would happen again.
And then they saw the
people going a w a y.
Cubby turned to his
mother. "This," he said,
"is what t h e giants
brought."

Old Faithful

"Yes, I think it is.
Never have I seen any-
thing more beautiful. I hope we may see it again before we go."

But now they were hungry, and in the darkness Cubby
and his mother visited the refuse pails around the cabins.
Once as Cubby was looking about for himself he rounded

the corner of a cabin and came face to face with a little girl and her mother.

"Shoo!" they said, boldly, and seemed quite pleased to think they were so brave. Cubby turned quickly and ran back the way he had come, but, there was another lady and she too said "Shoo!" He wanted to be a good little bear and please them all, so he turned and ran again around the corner, but there were the first little girl and her mother. This time they did not say, "Shoo!" They screamed and ran. Cubby became frightened and made a little cry in his throat, and in no time there was his mother!

"What is the matter?" she asked. "Did someone hurt you?"

And then Cubby laughed. It was funny now. He told his mother about it, and how both the ladies and the little girl had been so brave and then had grown so frightened.

"Why are they afraid of us?" he asked.

"Well, there are bears," said his mother, "who have bad tempers and get angry. Then they do things that hurt. People who keep a safe distance from bears are really the safest, for all bears cannot be trusted. But they seldom bother people if they are not bothered first."

The next morning Cubby and Mommie Bear saw the great column of water rise again, and learned that it was called a geyser. "That's a queer word," Cubby thought to himself. Then they saw a great many people gather together and set out on what they called a hike to see all the wonders. "Let us go too," said Mommie Bear. "See, one of our friends, the Ranger, is going with them. We may learn a great deal."

And so they went. And one of the things they learned was the name of the great geyser they had watched. It was Old Faithful, so named because it played regularly every hour, and could always be depended upon.

They were told what made the great wall of water rise. They were shown pretty pools of lovely colors filled with scalding hot water, and they watched other geysers play, some even larger than Old Faithful. The Ranger said there were sixty active ones in the Park, twelve of them larger than any others in all the world. Cubby and his mother and the people were very interested in all he had to tell them. When they came to a little bridge, the Ranger had the people counted as they walked across. There were just a hundred and ninety-seven people and a mother bear and her cub that morning.

CHAPTER XXIV

WHAT THE GIANTS FOUND

A T last when they were by themselves Cubby said, "Mommie Bear, tell me the rest of the story about the giants. I know that you can now."

"We will tell it together," said Mommie Bear. "When the great giants set out to find something very wonderful to bring back to Mother Nature's wonderland they made up their minds that they would bring something that was not to be found anywhere else in this country. They looked here and they looked there, but they could not seem to find it. The wonderland had mountains. There were mountains of glass and smoking mountains; there were springs and falls and lovely canyons. But they did not give up. And then, at last, in a far-away country called Iceland, they found something they had never seen before. It was a geyser. It would shoot a stream of boiling hot water with steam high, high into the air!

" 'How beautiful!' said the two giants, 'how lovely it would be if we could carry this to Mother Nature's wonderland!' So they thought about it and studied it and at last decided to make one like it.

"They came back to the wonderland and asked Mother Nature to turn them into two of her great nature giants so that they might be useful and make something lovely for all to see. Their home was to be deep in the earth.

"So Mother Nature turned them into two great giants, the giant heat and the giant water. They went to live in their home. At once they set about making the marvelous thing for the wonderland. The water lived in a narrow deep crevice in the earth and the heat had its home below. When the water at the bottom of the deep crevice became heated it turned to steam, then it was very, very strong. At last it would grow strong enough to raise the whole column of water above it and shoot it high in the sky. And then the steam would fly out in great clouds and rise up, up, up into the heavens, making rainbows in the rays of sunlight."

"Yes," said Cubby, "and then all the water that had run out would run back into its deep crevice and it would all happen over again!"

"You are right," said Mommie Bear. "People who came to the Park loved the geysers the best of all, and loved to watch them play. And so the giants brought something very wonderful to the wonderland."

"I like that story," said Cubby. "All the giants in nature are so wonderful. Let us go and watch Old Faithful again to-night."

"We will go first to the bear feeding grounds," said Mommie Bear. "Our friend the Ranger will be there again. There is a great sign that says 'Lunch Counter For Bears Only.' The people will come out to see us and they say the Ranger tells many interesting things about us and about other wild creatures in the Park."

They found several bears waiting when they arrived. The people had gathered and sat on low benches a safe distance away. And then a wagon loaded with things that bears like drove up and was emptied on their platform.

Cubby heard a great deal about himself. He had never known that he was so tiny when he was born—not much bigger than a squirrel.

"My, how I have grown!" he thought. "I'll be turning into that big bear before I know it."

It was fun hearing the Ranger tell how the Mommie Bears train their babies, even to spanking them when they are naughty. He was having a very interesting time when his mother said they should go.

It was growing dark and the grizzly bears were coming in. Cubby knew about them. They were larger than the black bears and more timid, but they were fierce fighters and Mommie Bear did not want to have any trouble with them.

"For all that they are a sort of cousin of ours," she told Cubby, "but we do not have much to do with one another. Our people are rather afraid of the grizzly. But he is a fine fellow. He lives much like we do on insects and plant food."

They found another crowd waiting to see Old Faithful play. As Cubby and Mommie sat and watched and wondered a voice beside them said: "I suppose people are more interested in these geysers than in anything else they see in the Park. To think that in all our great land this is the only place where we can see this wonderful act of nature!"

"They are marvelous," said another, "but there is something else here that interests the tourists very much. It's the bears. Everyone who comes is interested in them. I have read in books written by people who have lived here and know, that the tourists take more pictures of bears and talk more about them than about anything else."

"But look, there she goes, isn't it magnificent!" And the great column of water and cloud of steam shot straight through to the sky.

When it was over, Cubby turned to his mother. "Did you hear?" he whispered. "Do you suppose it was us that the giants brought to the Park?"

"Nonsense," said Mommie Bear. "How could anyone be interested in us when they can look at Old Faithful? But," and she smiled to herself, "I'm glad the people like us, and we surely do like the people."

CHAPTER XXV

GOING HOME

MOMMIE BEAR and Cubby stayed for many days at Old Faithful, for there was much to see. Cubby never tired of going every hour to watch Old Faithful perform. "It plays every hour," he said, "even when the world is frozen over and we are asleep."

"Yes," said his mother. "It is faithful. But we must be going on, Cubby. There are fine steam-heated dens here. I have talked to many bears who have slept in them, but do you know what I want to do?"

"Yes, Mommie Bear," said Cubby. "You want to go home."

"I want to go home," she repeated. "I feel the Old Teton Mountain calling to me. It is as though it held out its arms and said, 'Come my children, come and let me hold you safe!' I do not want to sleep in a steam-heated den."

Mommie looked this way and that. Then she sighed softly. "We will not have time to see it all, Cubby," she said, sadly. "I did hope that we could take the trail to the east entrance. They say it is so beautiful. Yonder are lovely lakes—just the kind bears like the best, filled with fish and set in the midst of deep forests with high mountain peaks around them. I did want to see the beautiful Sylvan Pass we have heard so much about and the many strange rock pictures."

"Oh, I wish we could go," said Cubby.

But Mommie Bear shook her head. "The rocks are shaped like many strange things," she said, thoughtfully. "I have heard of the Chimney Rock, Clock Tower, Elephant's Head, and many others. If we could go still farther, we would see two mountains that once were one before the Shoshone River cut its gorge through the rocky walls."

"The water is a giant," said Cubby, softly.

"And man is a giant too," said Mommie Bear. "Along the straight granite walls of this wonderful canyon he has cut a road with many tunnels through the solid rock. Across the river he has built a huge dam—"

"Like Bessie Beaver's?" Cubby interrupted.

"Oh, much larger," smiled his mother. "I have heard that it is even higher than the falls of the Yellowstone! We cannot see them this year, Cubby, dear. But we have all this to look forward to. Now we will go home and think over all that we have seen and dream over the beautiful things that we shall see next summer."

And so they set out together along the lovely road that led back to West Thumb on the Yellowstone Lake. Overhead great Vee-shaped flocks of birds were flying to the south.

"They are going home," said Mommie Bear.

Squirrels hurried by, with pine cones. "They are going home," said Cubby.

The woodchucks were leaving the lodges, going home for their long winter nap.

"Winter time is going-home time," said Mommie Bear; "even the tourists are going home."

The days had passed swiftly. Now the cold was in the air. Bits of white snow flitted down from the gray sky.

"And the snow is coming home," said Cubby, "coming to lie all winter over the plants and flowers that have gone to sleep."

It was as if everything sang, "We are going home, home, home."

At last the great peaks of the Tetons stood out like a blue cloud before them.

"They are calling us," said Mommie Bear. "Up there is our snug den. Our old mountain will hold us safe and warm until the spring comes again."

And at last, after a summer in wonderland, Cubby and his mother had come home.

Going home

CPSIA information can be obtained at www.ICGtesting.com
Printed in the USA
BVOW08s1844040316

439120BV00004B/29/P